UNDERSTANDING
ORGANIZATIONS
...FINALLY!

Structuring in Sevens

HENRY MINTZBERG

UNDERSTANDING ORGANIZATIONS ... FINALLY!

Berrett–Koehler Publishers, Inc.

Berrett-Koehler Publishers, Inc.
1333 Broadway, Suite 1000
Oakland, CA 94612-1921
Tel: (510) 817-2277 | Fax: (510) 817-2278
www.bkconnection.com

ORDERING INFORMATION

QUANTITY SALES. Special discounts are available on quantity purchases by corporations, associations, and others. For details, contact the "Special Sales Department" at the Berrett-Koehler address above.

INDIVIDUAL SALES. Berrett-Koehler publications are available through most bookstores. They can also be ordered directly from Berrett-Koehler: Tel: (800) 929-2929; Fax: (802) 864-7626; www .bkconnection.com.

ORDERS FOR COLLEGE TEXTBOOK / COURSE ADOPTION USE. Please contact Berrett-Koehler: Tel: (800) 929-2929; Fax: (802) 864-7626.

Distributed to the U.S. trade and internationally by Penguin Random House Publisher Services.

Berrett-Koehler and the BK logo are registered trademarks of Berrett-Koehler Publishers, Inc.

Printed in the United States of America

Berrett-Koehler books are printed on long-lasting acid-free paper. When it is available, we choose paper that has been manufactured by environmentally responsible processes. These may include using trees grown in sustainable forests, incorporating recycled paper, minimizing chlorine in bleaching, or recycling the energy produced at the paper mill.

Library of Congress Cataloging-in-Publication Data

Names: Mintzberg, Henry, author.
Title: Understanding organizations...finally! : structuring in sevens / Henry Mintzberg.
Description: First edition. | Oakland, CA : Berrett-Koehler Publishers, Inc. [2023] | Includes bibliographical references and index.
Identifiers: LCCN 2022025337 (print) | LCCN 2022025338 (ebook) | ISBN 9781523000050 (paperback ; alk. paper) | ISBN 9781523000067 (pdf) | ISBN 9781523000074 (epub) | ISBN 9781523000081
Subjects: LCSH: Industrial organization. | Management.
Classification: LCC HD31.2 .M564 2023 (print) | LCC HD31.2 (ebook) | DDC 658.4/02—dc23/ eng/20220609
LC record available at https://lccn.loc.gov/2022025337
LC ebook record available at https://lccn.loc.gov/2022025338

First Edition

30 29 28 27 26 25 24 23 22 | 10 9 8 7 6 5 4 3 2 1

Book producer and text designer: BookMatters
Cover designer: Daniel Tesser

To Dulcie . . . together, finally!

Contents

Preface

In 1979 I published *The Structuring of Organizations: A Synthesis of the Research*, 512 pages of small type. I like it best of all my books, for its flow and cohesion. It has also been my most successful book, especially in its shortened version, *Structure in Fives*, released in 1983, with 312 pages of larger type.

Here I revise and update that book, not as a synthesis of the research so much as a synthesis of my lifetime of experiences with organizations. In 1979 the published research required synthesis: there was a great deal of literature, but all over the place. These books pulled it together. But the need remains, in practice as well as education, for a wider understanding of organizations, which are central to almost everything we do.

So here, on the foundation of *Structure in Fives*, I pull together a half century of experience—my own and whatever else I found—as *Structuring in Sevens*, for the purposes of *Understanding Organizations ... Finally!*

Hermits can stop reading here. So can pedants: this book has fewer references, and I make no apologies for the many that are older. Good insights, like good wine, survive the test of time. So do good stories, of which you will read many old, as well as new.

I may be better known as a management theorist, but, more fundamentally, I am an organization theorist. Almost all my working life has been devoted to understanding these strange beasts. If a good chess player can go from one match to the next, understanding the board quickly, I feel that, with so many years observing, advising, and experiencing organizations, as soon as I enter one, I get a visceral sense of it—the culture, the condition, almost the smell of the place. Imagine how much experience, how many stories, can be accumulated in half a century. I heard once about a science-fiction character who went mad because every time he passed grass being cut, he could hear it screaming. I'm not going mad, but when I am near an organization, I can hear the screams—whether of delight or despair.

Books are written by individuals, but with the support of organizations (like most everything else these days). Thank you especially McGill University, for always being so supportive, likewise our current dean Yolande Chan, and Berrett-Koehler, for always being so engaging, especially Neal Maillet as a delightful partner on this book, as was Steve Piersanti on all the others.

The support of other individuals has been substantial, and heartfelt: Dulcie Naimer, who contributed so much, personally and materially; Santa Balanca-Rodrigues, who, after a quarter century, becomes a better assistant by the day; Jeremiah Lee, who set this book on course early; Jeff Kulick, who takes manuscript review to rare heights; Alex Anderson, whose meticulousness combined well with my lack of it; Charles Marful, who saved me from messing up Chapters 2–6; Lars Groth, whose detailed feedback helped to clarify several confusions; Saku Mantere, whose help on Chapter 20 was invaluable; the excellent work of David Peattie and Ashley Ingram in production, Amy Smith Bell for her careful editing, Susan Mintzberg for her unofficial editing, Dave Dudley for great diagrams, and for other specific help, Hanieh Mohammadi, Karl Moore, and P. D. Jose.

CHAPTER 1

Our World of Organizations

How many organizations are you connecting with today? Is ten an exaggeration? Let's start in the morning. First thing, you check your email, courtesy of a phone maker and an internet provider. Breakfast has been brought to you by farmers, factories, and food stores as well as airlines and truckers. Off you go to work in a business, government, or nongovernmental organization (NGO), or maybe to study in a school, transported by your local bus company, unless you drive on a road patrolled by the police and maintained by the municipality. Lunch in a cafeteria might be followed by a visit to your bank, or a workout at the gym. Back home, you check out some fact on Wikipedia, via Google, and then watch the news on a TV network, before reading this book produced for you by a publisher (and written by an author, but I am not an organization). I count at least fifteen: how many did I miss?

We live in a world of organizations, from our birth in hospitals until our burial by funeral homes. In between, we are educated, employed, entertained, and exasperated by organizations. Yet what do we really understand about them?

If you want to learn about yourself—your personality, your anxieties, whatever—walk into any bookstore and choose from among dozens of books on self-help. If you are concerned about the economy, read any number of political blogs to get the latest word. But **between our micro selves and our macro economies, where can we go to find out how these social things called organizations really work?** (Note that the main points of this book are highlighted in **bold face** type.)

Welcome to *Understanding Organizations ... Finally!*

What's an Organization Anyway?

A seven-year-old asks you: "What are these 'organizations' you keep talking about? What's a Google anyway? And how can an organization be an apple?" How do you answer? That it's a building? A logo on the paychecks of the people called *employees*? You can see a whole apple in a supermarket, but where can you go to see the whole of this Apple? Welcome all seven-year-olds and adults to the woolly world of organizations.

A COUPLE OF DEFINITIONS

Let's get a bit formal before we continue:

An organization can be defined as collective action structured for the pursuit of a common mission. To put this for seven-year-olds and everyone older, a number of people work in some formalized arrangement to accomplish something. And **the structure of an organization can be defined as the pattern of relationships designed to enable its people to take that action together.**

Let's start with a big picture: the immense variety of organizations out there. Figure 1.1 organizes organizations according to the sector in which they work: public sector governments, private sector businesses, and plural sector associations, most community based (and owned by members, as are cooperatives, or else by no one, as in, charities, NGOs, and *private* universities).[1] You probably know something about many that are listed, but here they are altogether:

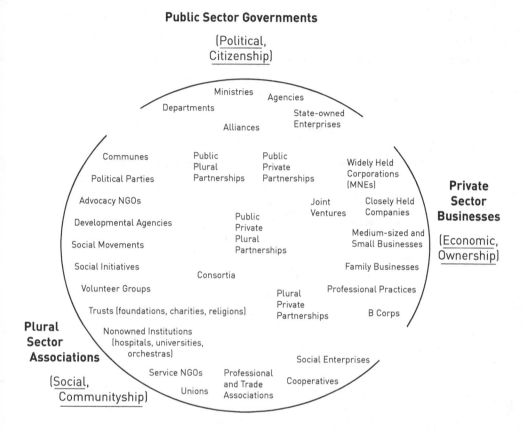

Public Sector Governments

(Political, Citizenship)

Ministries
Agencies
Departments
State-owned Enterprises
Alliances

Communes
Public Plural Partnerships
Public Private Partnerships
Widely Held Corporations (MNEs)

Political Parties

Advocacy NGOs
Joint Ventures
Closely Held Companies

Developmental Agencies
Public Private Plural Partnerships
Medium-sized and Small Businesses

Social Movements

Social Initiatives
Family Businesses

Consortia

Volunteer Groups
Professional Practices
Plural Private Partnerships

Trusts (foundations, charities, religions)
B Corps

Nonowned Institutions (hospitals, universities, orchestras)

Social Enterprises

Service NGOs
Professional and Trade Associations
Cooperatives

Unions

Private Sector Businesses

(Economic, Ownership)

Plural Sector Associations

(Social, Communityship)

FIGURE 1.1 **Mapping Our World of Organizations**

The One Worst Way to Organize

In 1911 Frederick Taylor wrote a book called *Principles of Scientific Management* that proposed the "one best method"—now known as the "one best way"—to manage work in every organization.[2] The way he proposed has mostly been forgotten: to stand over workers with a stopwatch and microanalyze every detail of their work, treating them as hands without heads. But not forgotten is the idea that there is always some best way or other—for repair shops and automobile companies alike, food banks and factory farms. (Strategic Planning, everyone?) **Believing there is one best way to structure organizations**

is the worst way to manage them. Organizations vary immensely. For example, you may have noticed that a symphony orchestra is different from a factory. Well, not all of us have (see box).

AN EFFICIENT ORCHESTRA

A young business school student finally got the chance to apply his learning. He was asked to select an organization about which he had no familiarity, to study it, and make recommendations to improve its efficiency. He chose a symphony orchestra, attended his first concert, and submitted the following analysis:

a. For considerable periods the four oboe players had nothing to do. The number of oboes should therefore be reduced, and the work spread more evenly over the whole concert program, thus eliminating the peaks and valleys of activity.

b. All twenty violins were playing identical notes. This would seem to be an unnecessary duplication, so the staff of this section should be cut drastically.

c. Obsolescence of equipment is another matter warranting further investigation. The program noted that the leading violinist's instrument was several hundred years old. If normal depreciation schedules had been applied, the value of this instrument would have been reduced to zero and the purchase of more modern equipment recommended long ago.

d. Much effort was absorbed in the playing of demisemiquavers, which seems to be an unnecessary refinement. It is recommended that all notes be rounded up to the nearest semiquaver. If this were done, it would be possible to use trainees and lower-grade operatives more extensively.

e. Finally, there seemed to be too much repetition of some of the musical passages. Therefore, scores should be pruned to a considerable extent. No useful purpose is served by repeating on the horns something which has already been handled by the strings. It is estimated that, if all redundant passages were eliminated, the whole concert time of two hours could be reduced to twenty minutes and there would be no need for an intermission.[3]

This is funny, right? But what if this student chose to study a factory instead? No one would be laughing, least of all its workers. This story is, of course, apocryphal—but only with regard to context. Stories like this abound. One Harvard Business School professor delighted in describing hospitals as "focused factories."[4] Is this where you would like to have your baby delivered? And how about the many politicians who believe that government should be run like a business? Should business be run like a government? Should soccer (football) in Europe be played with the equipment of football in North America?[5]

Biggest, Boldest, Smallest, Strangest

What's the biggest organization you can think of? My choice is not quite the biggest so much as the boldest. The National Health Service of England has boasted of being surpassed in size only by the Chinese Red Army, Walmart, and the Indian Railroad. Some standards! Is this the mind-set you want from that physician who will be delivering your baby?

What's the smallest? I discovered this early, working for a tiny tag and label company. It had two managers: one for production, the other for sales. They couldn't figure out why the order dockets took so long to get into production, so I tracked them—kind of in Taylor's way. A docket sat on the desk of one of the managers until he signed it, then on the desk of the other until he signed it, then back to the first. The moral of the story is that two managers are more than enough to make a bureaucracy.

What's the strangest organization you can think of? How about the Paperweight Collectors Association, or the Association of Association Executives? Some years ago, I came across the Flying Funeral Directors of America, with the stated mission "to create and further common interest in flying and funeral services; to join together in master disaster, and to improve flying safety."[6] Some mission: they couldn't decide whether to bury the passengers or save them.

And what's the most common organization? Restaurants, perhaps: there's probably one around the corner from you. Yet think about how even restaurants vary—from greasy spoons to fast-food franchises to gourmet dining rooms to caterers of events. We can no more find one best way to structure all these restaurants than can we find one best chef to cook in all of them.

Organization No-Speak

Two Canadian biologists meet to discuss their research. One has been studying bears, the other beavers. But let's assume that they have no such vocabulary—no words for these different species—only the word *mammal*, much the way we use the word *organization*. They get into a discussion about where is the best place for a mammal to spend the winter.

"In a cave, of course," says the bear biologist.

"Are you kidding?" says the beaver biologist. "Their predators will come in and eat them. They have to build a wooden structure by the side of a lake so they can swim into it safely."

"Now you're the one who's kidding," retorts the bear biologist. "Mammals don't have predators!"

They talk past each other because of the limitations of their vocabulary, just as we talk past each other because **we lack vocabulary to discuss species of organizations.** That's how orchestras get confused with factories. Ignorance is our predator: it devours our organizations by ignoring their differences. This book provides a vocabulary to get past that.

Fives to Sevens (and Beyond)

In 1983 I published *Structure in Fives*, which was a shorter version of *The Structuring of Organizations: A Synthesis of the Research*, published in 1979.[7] Recently I felt the time has come to revise it, as a synthesis of a half century of experience with organizations, especially to extend the five forms that were the basis of that book to seven, alongside seven forces that lie at the heart of structuring organizations (see box).

THE MAGIC NUMBER SEVEN

According to the *Dictionnaire des Symboles*, "five is the number of the center, of harmony and equilibrium."[8] Maybe so, but seven is the number of "perfection," the "symbol of human totality," thus of completion. So why not seven here?

In a famous article titled "The Magic Number Seven, Plus or Minus Two," the psychologist George Miller suggested that our inclination to classify things into sevens (the seven wonders of the world, the seven days of the week, etc.) reflects the number of "chunks" of information that we are able to retain in our short- and medium-term memories.[9] Three wonders of the world would fall a little flat, so to speak, while twelve would be daunting. So why not seven for our world of organizations? After all, I don't want to overload you as a reader, any more than myself as a writer. (At least until we get to Chapter 17.)

As I began this book, I had a chat with Jeremiah Lee, a consultant friend in Boston who knows much of my work well. He asked a question that took this book to another place. Since a number of my other books were written as syntheses (about strategy, managerial work, and balance in society), he asked how about a synthesis of these syntheses.[10] Hence I decided (a) to rename the main title *Understanding Organization...Finally!* (b) to bring together an understanding of managing, decision making, and strategy formation around the central issues of organizing; and (c) to do all this in a much more spirited tone, in an effort to reach everyone who needs to understand organizations. (How am I doing so far?)

As you might have guessed, there are seven parts in this book. After "Re-Viewing the Organization" in Part I, to see it more insightfully, including how it uses art, craft, and science to make decisions, create strategies, and conduct management, Part II introduces the basic building blocks of organization design, which Part III assembles into four fundamental forms of organization (Personal, Programmed, Professional, and Project). These constitute the core of the book.

Beyond a set of forms, we need to see organizing as a web of forces. Accordingly, Part IV introduces four basic forces (consolidation, efficiency, proficiency, and collaboration), one of which predominates in each of the four forms, and three additional forces that can be prevalent in all of the forms (the overlay of separation, the infusion of culture, and the intrusion of conflict). These three forces, in turn, suggest three more forms (Divisional Form, Community Ship, and Political Arena), which are described in Part V, thus leaving us up with seven forms and seven forces.

Part VI weaves these forces through the forms, to describe how they anchor the forms to prevent them from going out of control, establish hybrids of them, and drive transitions across the life cycle of organizations.

Part VII closes the book by opening it up, beyond sevens, by showing first, how organizations have been opening their borders, to go outward bound, and second, how the process of structuring the organization can be opened up, to design doing.

Hermits may not need to understand organizations, but the rest of us do, at least if we are to make constructive use of them. What are these beasts? How do they work? When don't they work? How can we make them work better? The answers are important because, as soon as you put down this book, you will be facing the bears, beavers, and other beasts of our world of organizations. Help is on the way!

PART I

RE-VIEWING
THE ORGANIZATION

Walk into an organization and ask to see a picture of it. Chances are they will show you "The Chart." Is there no more to the place than the stacking of one boss atop another? It's like visiting friends, and, asking to see the family album, they show you the family tree.

It is time to re-view our organizations. Chapter 2 considers who players in the organization are, and where. And Chapter 3 uses a triangle of art, craft, and science to illustrate various ways in which decisions are made, strategies form, and managers get their work done in organizations.

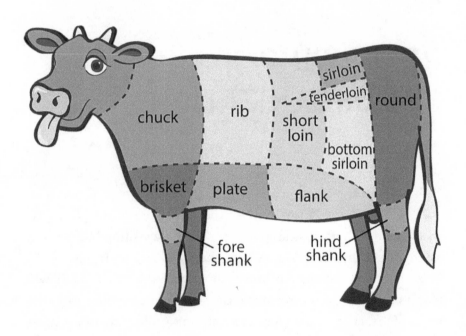

CHAPTER 2

The Players and the Parts

An ad appeared some years ago for a major software company that showed a drawing similar to the one here, claiming that this is not a cow because it is a chart of the parts of a cow. In a healthy cow the parts don't even know that they are parts; they just work together harmoniously. The ad asked **would you like your organization to work like a chart or a cow?**[11]

This is a serious question! Cows have no trouble working like cows, nor, for that matter, do any of us working as individual human beings, physiologically at least. So why do we have so much trouble working together socially? Is it because we are so obsessed with those charts?

Thinking Outside the Boxes

We talk incessantly about "thinking outside the box," from inside our boxes, especially that chart (Figure 2.1). (It was first used in the eighteenth century and has been unstoppable ever since.)

Is its chart the organization? Is its skeleton the cow? Are the boxes of the chart the managers of the organization, and the lines between them their conversations? Or do these boxes just box us all in?

Of course, the chart has its uses. Like a map that identifies the

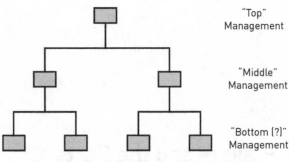

FIGURE 2.1 An Organization

towns, and the roads that connect them, the chart shows us how the parts and people are grouped into units, and how these are connected through formal authority—in other words, who reports to whom, and with what title. But just as a map fails to tell us about the economy and the society, so the chart fails to tell us how things happen in the organization, let alone why. Sometimes you can't even tell from the chart what the place does for a living. What the chart certainly shows is that we are obsessed with authority, seduced by status—who's on top and all that (see box).

ON TOP OF WHAT?

We use the term *top management* rather casually. On top of what? The chart, to be sure, the salary scale too, maybe even the headquarters building. But does seeing oneself on top of an organization enable a chief to be on top of what is going on in that organization? Hardly, with everyone else seen as below.

Under this top management is the *middle management*. In the middle of the chart, to be sure, but in the middle of what is going on in the organization? There are middle managers who just pass information down and up the hierarchy, while others manage to connect the actions on the ground with the abstractions in the offices. Maybe, then, we should be calling these people *connecting managers*.

And how about *bottom management*? Have you ever heard that term? Surely, if there are top managers and middle managers, there must be

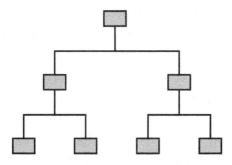

FIGURE 2.2 **A reorganization**

bottom managers too, right there on the bottom of the chart. While no organization may use this term, every bottom manager knows exactly where he or she sits in the chart, if not, hopefully, in the organization.

If you would like to fix these distortions in your own organization, let me suggest that you ban the term *top management* until you are prepared to use the term *bottom management*.

Here Comes Yet Another Reorganization Now have a look at Figure 2.2, compared with Figure 2.1. It shows a reorganization. Did you notice the difference? The managers who have been shuffled around the chart certainly do: each has a new title, or a new "superior," or some new "subordinates." (What awful terms.) There must be more to organizations than all this labeling and bossing. If seeing is believing, we had better see our organizations differently.

Reorganizing is so popular in organizations because it's so easy. All you need is a piece of paper and a pen—better still a pencil, with a good eraser, if not a screen with a great big DELETE button. Accounting goes here, marketing goes there, and so on. Travis becomes the Minister of Transport, Daphne becomes the Minister of Defense. Off they all go...into utter confusion. "We have trained hard, but it seemed that every time we were beginning to form up into teams, we would be re-organized. I was to learn later in life that we tend to meet any new situation by re-organization: and what a wonderful method it can be for creating the illusion of progress while producing confusion, inefficiency, and demoralization." (This is usually attributed to Petronius Arbiter of the Roman Navy, 250 BC, but, apparently, was actually written around 1948.)

Imagine, instead, an architectural reorganization: shuffling where people sit. This may take more effort, for the designers at least, but it can result in less effort for everyone else. Suddenly Enid from Engineering finds herself sitting next to Max from Marketing. Rather than continuing to complain about each other, now they talk to each other—at the coffee machine, at least. No boss in sight. That's a reorganization!

The Principal Players

Cows have real parts, like lungs and livers, brains and bowels. These do real things (compared with a sirloin steak, which does nothing for a cow, except end its life). Organizations, likewise, have real parts, with players who do real things. Here are the main ones.

- The *operators* **do the basic operating work of the organization: producing the products, rendering the customer services, and whatever supports these directly.** On a hockey team they score the goals, stop the shots, maintain the equipment. In a restaurant they serve the sirloins and park the Passats. In manufacturing companies they are the purchasing agents, machine operators, salespeople, and so on.

- The *support staff* **support the operations indirectly.** They develop the information systems, provide the legal services, welcome visitors at the reception. Count all the support services in a university—libraries, placement, payroll, residences, alumni relations, human resources, faculty club, and many more—so many that you have to wonder if there's any room left for the professors. (The term *staff* is used in other ways as well, sometimes for employees in general, such as the staff of a law office, for certain operators, including physicians in hospitals, even for the senior management, as in the chief of staff in the military.)

- **The *analysts* use analysis to control and adapt the activities in one way or another: they plan them, schedule them, measure them, budget them, and sometimes train the people who do them—they just don't do them themselves.** Together, these analysts are sometimes referred to as the *technostructure* of the organization. As we shall see, some organizations have hardly any analysts and support staff while others are inundated with one or both.

- **The *managers* oversee all this, having formal responsibility for some particular unit in the organization, or the whole of it.** A *unit* is some part of the organization designated in its formal structure: an emergency room in a hospital, a pastry kitchen in a restaurant, a forward line in hockey. In all but the smallest organizations, these units are usually shown in the chart stacked upon each other to form the *official hierarchy of authority*. Soldiers are thus grouped into squads, squads into platoons, and on into companies, battalions, brigades, and divisions, until the final grouping into armies. Each has its own manager, from sergeant to general. Elsewhere, we find managers with titles such as coach in hockey, bishop in religion, director of a film. The manager in charge of a whole business is usually called chief executive officer (CEO), to whom may report various other members of the *C-suite*: COO (operating), CFO (finance), CLO (learning), and so on. Now, aping business, CEOs are springing up in all kinds of other organizations. (At least the head of the Roman Catholic Church is still called Pope.) All managers, beyond overseeing the work of their unit, connect it to the outside world. A sales manager meets customers; the Pope addresses the faithful in Saint Peter's Square.

- **The *culture* is the system of beliefs that permeates the organization, providing a common frame for all the players, ideally to breathe some life into the skeleton of the structure.** Just as every person has a personality, so too does every organization have a culture, its way of doing things, ranging from rather indistinct to highly compelling. (Beyond this, we find cultures in occupations, such as medicine, in functions within an organization, say sales compared with marketing, and, of course, in nations, say German compared with Italian.) For many years, Ed Schein has described organizational culture on three levels.[12] At the surface are the *artifacts* that symbolize the place visibly (the Apple logo on a laptop, the cross for the Catholic Church, the Statue of Liberty for the United States). A bit deeper are the *espoused values*, public statements of intent (the Ten Commandments or some other mission statement). And most deeply embedded, sometimes unconscious, are the *basic assumptions* that can be found in the behaviors of the players (maintaining top quality, get everything done quickly). Of course, in a healthy organization the espoused values are manifested in the basic assumptions, but not always. For example, *greenwashing* is the name given to empty statements about responsibility to the environment.

- **The external *influencers* seek to shape the behavior of the organization from the outside**, for example, the unions, local communities, and other special interest groups that lobby the big corporations and these corporations themselves that lobby governments. Greenpeace lobbies at the COP (UN climate change) conferences, and the Rio de Janeiro fans support the Flamengo team. Many of the influencers of businesses are now referred to as *stakeholders*, in contrast to the owners of the stock, who are called *shareholders*.[13] Together, all these influencers form an *external coalition* that may be *passive*, actively *dominated* by one group, or *divided* among several.[14]

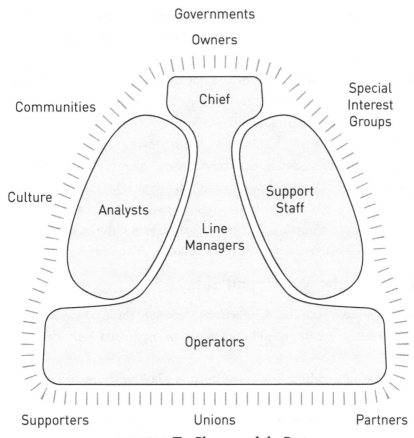

FIGURE 2.3 **The Players and the Parts**

An Earlier Logo

Books are written in linear order, every single word in a single sequence, from beginning to end. This may be fine for a diary, but in other books, this linear order has to describe something that is not linear at all—here, the nature of organizations. Diagrams, figures, and other images can help us to see past this, by illustrating the woven reality. So be prepared for many images.

For the original version of this book, I created a diagram to locate these players (Figure 2.3). The operators were put at the base and the line managers—bottom to middle to top (called *strategic apex*)—were put above them, with the analysts and support staff to either side. Later I added *culture* as a kind of halo, and the *influencers*, all around. This became a kind of logo for the book, and people had a field day with what they saw: lungs, a fly's head, a kidney bean, female ovaries, an upside-down mushroom, and worse.

When I began work on this new edition, however, I realized that in this figure I had acceded to the conventional, hierarchical view of the organization. But instead of dropping the logo from this book, I decided to drop the hierarchy in the logo, as you will see by shaping it in various ways to demonstrate how organizations differ, some looking more like the original drawing, others flatter, or rounder.

Chains, Hubs, Webs, and Sets

Now let's look at some connections between the parts, as chains, hubs, webs, and sets, to help explain how organized activities flow, or don't.

Consider a wedding. The event itself is a *hub*, with the guests coming from different places to a central place. As the diners line up at a buffet table, they form a *chain*, advancing in single file from one dish to the next. Then they take their seats at a table, one of a *set* of them around the room. When the dancing starts, however, the place becomes a *web* of interactive activity, as the guests chat and move every which way.

Seeing the Organization as a Chain

These days, the most popular depiction of the organization is as **a chain, where**  **work is seen to flow in a linear sequence**. For example, automobiles are assembled as they move down the *line*, with the parts being added one after another. And how about a double play in baseball: from shortstop to second base to first base.

Michael Porter popularized the *value chain* as the common way to organize.[15] *Supply chain* has also come into popular usage, to describe logistics in organizations. But while books may be linear, much that goes on in organizations is not. In universities, do professors of strategy connect in any kind of chain with their colleagues in marketing? How about pediatrics and geriatrics in a hospital? (A long chain indeed.) Do the stores of even a *retail chain* work as a chain? Maybe, therefore, it's time to break the chain—into hubs, webs, and sets.

Seeing the Organization as a Hub

A hub is a coordinating center, a focal point of activity. We call an airport a hub when it is used extensively to transfer passengers between flights. But every airport is itself a hub to which flights and passengers come and from which they go, likewise a hospital for the patients and the staff. Indeed, within the hospital, for the most part, each patient is a hub. Rather than moving them around, most of their services—nursing, medical, food, oxygen—come to them. Likewise with the assembly of large aircraft: it can be easier to move the parts to the plane than the plane to the parts.[16] Even a manager can be seen as a hub: watch a football coach during practice.

Seeing the Organization as a Web

Visit the design studio of an architectural firm and, like those dancers at the wedding, you will find people interacting in all kinds of ways, not in the neat order of a chain or 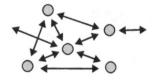 the focused flow of a hub. **Webs, or networks, are open-ended movement of people, information, and/or materials, with no fixed sequence or center.** They move flexibly, variably. When you don't quite know where you are going (unlike that double play in baseball), or where the center is (unlike that patient), but you do need to work closely together, you had better organize as a web. This is why the World Wide Web is called a web.

Seeing the Organization as a Set

But what happens when people don't have to
work closely together—say, across pediatrics
and geriatrics in the hospital, strategy and
marketing in the business school, even the
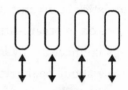
divisions—appropriately named—in a conglomerate company, let
alone the stores of a retail chain. Hardly a hub, a chain, even a web.
**But a set: The parts are "loosely coupled," barely connecting with
each other.** They share common resources. (Hence the university
has been defined as a collection of professors who share a parking
lot.)

Even when it may look like they are working together, these people
may be working apart. Watch an open-heart surgery (as a doctoral
student of mine once did, for five hours): the surgeon and the an-
esthesiologist may not exchange a single word. That is because each
knows exactly what to expect of the other. Or how about an orchestra during performance? The players barely look at the conductor, let
alone each other.

Lise Lamothe, who studied medical specialties in her doctoral the-
sis, found that cataract surgery worked like a chain of steps, rheu-
matology more like a hub (with the treating physician seeking con-
sultations from other specialists), and geriatrics like a web (where
teamwork is required for the multiplicity of disorders—one chief of
geriatrics in a Montreal hospital used to claim that a physiotherapist
was their best diagnostician).[17] Of course, all together in a hospital
they constitute a set.

For some years, when I wanted to understand how a particular organization worked, holistically, I brought together a few of
its people to draw an *organigraph*: a depiction of how work flows
through the place, identifying the role of each of its major players.
The notions of chains, hubs, webs, and sets were particularly helpful
for this.[18]

Where to See the Manager?

Looking back at the diagrams of the chain, hub, web, and set, ask yourself where to see the manager of each?

In a *chain,* the answer seems obvious. On top. **On top of the horizontal chain of operations is built the vertical *chain of command***—a manager for each link and a manager for all managers. So the chart does have its place after all (as we shall see in Chapter 8), however limited that may be (as we shall see in Chapters 7, 9, and 10).

In a hub, however, a manager who is on top of it is out of it (in both senses of the term). **The manager has to be in the center, where the action is.** Perhaps that is why the executive directors of hospitals (hubs) tend to be located on the main floor, whereas the CEOs of mass production (chain) corporations tend to sit on the top floor. About women managers, in *The Female Advantage: Women's Ways of Leadership,* Sally Helgesen wrote that they "usually referred to themselves as being in the middle of things. Not on top, but in the center, not reaching down, but reaching out."[19]

In a hub you can replace top, middle, and bottom management with concentric circles: put the chief in the *center,* surrounded by *connecting* managers, who link to the *operating* managers facing the surrounding world (Figure 2.4).

In a *web,* however, if you put the manager in the center, you "centralize" it—that is, turn it into a hub. Instead of people interacting every which way, they focus on the boss. Put its manager, instead, on top of a web and, again, you take him or her out of it. **So where to find the manager in a web? Everywhere—along every line and at all the nodes.** In other words, they have to get out of their offices and sit in on all sorts of meetings, join various conversations in the halls, experience what's happening on the ground. Not to micromanage, but to know what's going on and thus be ready to act when something goes wrong.

Steve Jobs spent his mornings in a design lab at Apple.[20] What

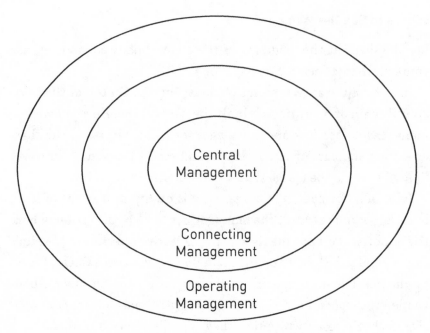

FIGURE 2.4 **Managing Around**

was the CEO of this huge, high-tech company doing there, instead of reading financial statements in his office like a proper CEO? He was using his best talent to help create more shareholder value than had any other company in history, including all those run by the number crunchers.

Moreover, in a web, managing can be, not only everywhere, but everyone. All kinds of players can perform tasks that are normally carried out by the managers who sit atop the chains or at the center of the hubs. (We shall return to this *distributed management* later in the book.)

In a *set*, with the people working largely on their own, the managers not only can be out of it, but may do better by largely *staying out of it*—instead exercising oversight. For example, no surgeon in an operating room relies on a manager to give instructions or otherwise to exercise control. Once the resources are allocated (say, in the form of budgets), people know what they have to do and just get on doing it.

So let's not tie all our hubs, webs, and sets in chains: all four of these are different yet legitimate ways to see and manage organizations. With these re-views of the parts and the players completed, let's turn now to some of the main processes in organizations.

CHAPTER 3

The Art, Craft, and Science of Organizing

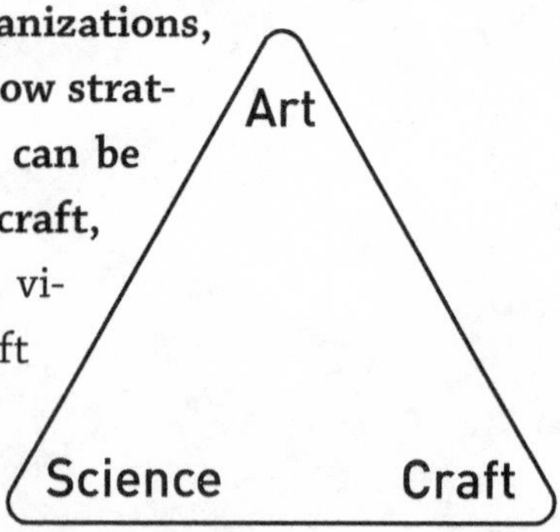

Much that is consequential in organizations, including how decisions are made, how strategies form, and what managers do, can be described at the interface of art, craft, and science. Art is based on insight, vision, intuition, and is idea-based. Craft is practical, realistic, engaging, and experience-based, while science is inclined to be more factual and analytical, evidence-based. You might wish to consider yourself in these terms before we discuss their use in decision making, strategy formation, and managerial work (see box).

(A triangle diagram with "Art" at the top, "Science" at the bottom left, and "Craft" at the bottom right is positioned in the upper right of the text.)

WHO DO YOU THINK YOU ARE?

Figure 3.1 lists various words across three columns down ten rows. Beverly Patwell, an organization development consultant, and I developed this to help people consider themselves, or others they know, as inclined to favor art, craft, and/or science.

On a paper copy or an electronic screen, in each of the ten rows, you can circle or highlight one of the three entries that best describes how you see yourself—as a manager, a person, whatever you wish. Just one entry on each line, please—the first thing that comes to your mind. Then add up the choices in each of the three columns: together, they should come to ten.

a. Circle one entry in each row

Ideas	Experiences	Facts
Intuitive	Practical	Analytical
Heart	Hands	Head
Strategies	Processes	Outcomes
Inspiring	Engaging	Informing
Passionate	Helpful	Reliable
Novel	Realistic	Determined
Imagining	Learning	Organizing
Seeing It	Doing It	Thinking It
"The possibilities are endless!"	"Consider it done!"	"That's perfect!"
TOTALS:		

b. Add total circles per column   Source: © Mintzberg and Patwell.

FIGURE 3.1 Describing Yourself

The first column gives your score for art, the second for craft, the third for science. On the triangle in Figure 3.2, choose the horizontal line labeled A (for art) that corresponds to your score in the first column. Then do the same for your score in the second column on the diagonal line marked C (for craft). Where these two lines meet (shown in the example on the upper right as 7 for A and 2 for C) should also be where your score falls on the S line (for science), to make a total of ten (hence S equals 1 in the example). This point on the triangle is how you see yourself with regard to art, craft, and science, whether oriented strongly to one or else to some combination of two or three.

Remember that these are your own perceptions. Other people may see you differently. You might even see yourself differently if you were in a different job, or living the life you dream of. If you work in a team, or live in a family, it can also be revealing to have everyone do this for

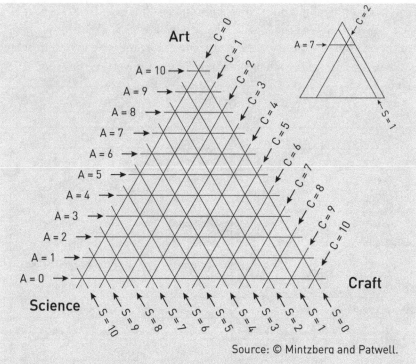

Source: © Mintzberg and Patwell.

FIGURE 3.2 **Positioning Yourself**

themselves and each other and compare the results. As we shall discuss later, while all kinds of people can be found in most organizations, one orientation sometimes dominates certain organizations. For example, we might expect many artists in advertising agencies, more craftspeople in engineering departments, and lots of science-oriented analysts in accounting firms.

Decision Making as Art, Craft, or Science

Decision making may not be what you think. It can also be what you see, and what you do. The analytical people are inclined to think first, the artists to see first, the craftspeople to do first.

We are all well versed in the steps necessary to make a decision:

define and diagnose the issue, find or create alternative courses of action to deal with it, evaluate each, and choose the best. If you *think* it's that simple, please consider perhaps the most important decision in your life—to find a mate. Is this what you did, or plan to do: identify the characteristics you are looking for in that special person, say, smart, stunning, serious; identify the available candidates; assess each on these characteristics; add up all these assessments to make the decision; and inform the lucky gal or guy? This is *thinking first*. It may sound sensible, but it doesn't always work, for mating and much else. If you tried this in your love life, you might still be single. ("What, you chose me? While you were going through this rigmarole, I got married and had a baby.")

More common in mating is *seeing first*, better known as "love at first sight": you turn a corner, see that special person, and that's that. *Seeing first* is likewise a lot more widespread in organizations than most people *think*—for example, in choosing someone for a job (*selection* at first sight).

And so is *doing first*. For its use in mating, I'll leave the details to your imagination (at least if you scored high on art). Let me just say that here, you do not think to do so much as do to think. Not being sure how to proceed, you try something, meet someone—take a little step—and if that works, you take a bigger step. If it doesn't, you try something else until something finally does work, and you do more of it. We find doing first, like the other two, in most every organization, although one or another may be favored, sometimes to excess. I once heard the definition of an actuary as someone who would have been an accountant but couldn't stand the excitement. In an advertising agency, however, you can have too much excitement. And how about excessive doing first: To quote Terry Connolly, a professor interested in decision making: "Nuclear wars and childbearing decisions are poor settings for a strategy of 'try a little one and see how it goes!'"[21]

Strategy Formation as Craft plus Art with Little Science

Strategy is a word that we always define in one way yet often use in another.[22] When I have asked groups of managers to define the word *strategy*, what I heard were words like *target*, *direction*, *vision*, most of all, *plan*. All describe strategy as *intended*—looking ahead—just as the

word is defined in the dictionary (Figure 3.3a). Then when I asked them to describe the strategy that their organization has actually been pursuing in recent years—namely, to look at strategy backward, as *realized*—they have always been happy to answer, in di-

FIGURE 3.3a **Strategy as Plan (intended)**

rect violation of the definitions they just gave (Figure 3.3b). We may think of strategy as plan ahead, yet we also see it as pattern behind, namely some consistency in what the organization actually did, for example, to go up-market with higher-quality products.

Finally, when I asked these groups of managers whether the strategy realized was intended, surprisingly few said yes or no. Most have seen it as a mixture of the two. As shown in Figure 3.4, **intended strategies that are realized can be called** *deliberate*, **and realized**

FIGURE 3.3b **Strategy as Pattern (realized)**

strategies that were not intended can be called *emergent*: **the organization made its way to the strategy action by action.**

Apparently, then, few strategies are purely deliberate or purely emergent. Most combine the two. And why not? **Organizations don't**

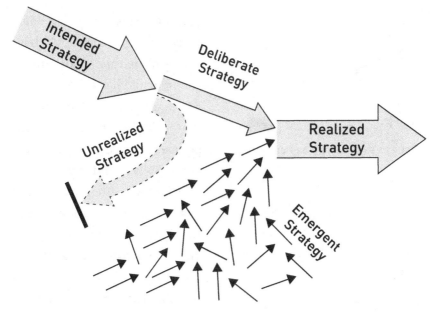

FIGURE 3.4 Forms of Strategy

just plan, they learn. They don't just think to get strategy; they
also do in order to see strategy. Strategy is about synthesis, and
you don't get synthesis from analysis. Analysis can help, but as an
input, not *the* process.

We can enlarge this picture of strategy by adding two more definitions, with regard to its content. When I have asked these groups
of managers whether Egg McMuffin—the American breakfast in a
bun—was a strategic change for McDonald's, they inevitably split.
Some say, *Of course, it was a new product in a new market*, while others
say, *Oh come on, it's the same old thing, just with new ingredients*. Both
are right; they just see the content of strategy differently.

Strategy can be a position in the marketplace (Figure 3.5a), as
Michael Porter would have it, **or a perspective of the organization,
its vision** (Figure 3.5b), what Peter Drucker called the "concept of the
corporation."[23] Egg McMuffin added a new position within the existing perspective. (Offering McDuckling à l'orange would have changed

FIGURE 3.5a **Strategy as Position**

FIGURE 3.5b **Strategy as Perspective**

both, while serving Big Macs on sourdough buns would have changed neither. Most interesting would have been serving Big Macs at the table, because that would have changed the perspective to maintain the position. Why would any company do that? Ask a newspaper that has lost so much readership to the blogs and streaming services. They have had to change how they do business in order to retain the same customers.)

Putting these four definitions of strategy together gives us four processes for creating it, which, as we shall see, map surprisingly well onto the four fundamental forms of organizations that we discuss in Part III: one for science, called *planning*, based on thinking, especially analyzing; one for art, based on seeing, called *visioning*; and two for craft, based on doing, called *venturing* and *learning*.

- The **planning model** postulates that strategies are formulated as deliberate positions by senior management, with the support of staff planners, to be implemented by everyone else.

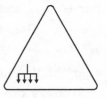

- The **visioning model** sees strategy as deliberate perspective, created in the mind of a visionary who has deep experience and creative insights. Within this vision, detailed strategic positions can emerge.

- The **venturing model** suggests that a thousand strategic positions bloom, so to speak, in the form of new ventures championed by all sorts of people and groups in the organization. These positions may be deliberate for them, but can be emergent—that is, unexpected—for the rest of the organization.

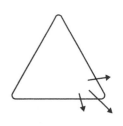

- The **learning model** is about doing first: strategic positions and perspective emerge through a process of trial-and-error learning, as active and informed individuals all over the organization reinforce each other's successes.

Managing as *Craft*, with *Art*, but Limited *Science*

If you ask what managers do, the answer will likely be that they plan, organize, coordinate, command and control. As noted earlier, these five words, all about control, date back to 1916. Watch what a manager does, any manager, and try to relate this to what you see going on.[24]

Management is a practice, not a profession or a science.[25] It is learned largely through experience, which means that it is primarily a craft, although some of the best managers make considerable use of art. They also use some science, in the form of analysis, but nowhere near as much as in the professions of medicine and engineering. The overuse of science, especially in an obsessive reliance on measurement, has become the scourge of "modern" management.

What, then, do managers really do? Following the early view as *controlling* have been a variety of others. Tom Peters described good managing as *doing*. ("'Don't think, do' is the phrase I favor"). On Wall Street, of course, managers *do deals*. In contrast, Michael Porter favored *thinking*, in particular "a set of analytical techniques for developing strategy."[26] (Hence, we can distinguish Porterian effectiveness—doing the right things—from Peterian effectiveness—doing

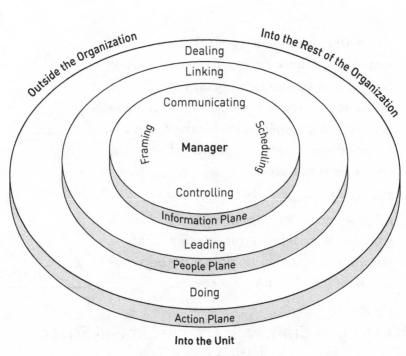

FIGURE 3.6 A Model of Managing

things right.) Both Warren Bennis and Abraham Zaleznik built their reputations among managers by claiming that *leading*, beyond simply managing, is what really matters,[27] whereas Herbert Simon built his reputation among academics by focusing on *decision making*.[28]

Each is wrong because all are right. **Managing is controlling and deciding, doing and dealing, thinking and leading, and more, not added up, but blended together.** The model of managing in Figure 3.6 shows the job comprehensively, on three rounded planes—information, people, and action—with the manager in the middle, between the unit managed and the rest of the organization as well as the outside world. Two roles can be described on each plane.

Managing on the Information Plane

On the information plane, managers use information to help people take action, in the roles of communicating and controlling.

- **Communication all around.** Watch any manager and one thing becomes readily apparent: the great amount of time spent simply communicating—namely, gathering and disseminating information—within the unit and around it.

- **Controlling inside.** A direct use of the manager's information is to steer the behavior of people in the unit. Not all of managing is about controlling, but some of it is, through the exercise of formal authority.

Managing on the People Plane

To manage *with* people, instead of *through* information, is to move closer to action, by helping other people make things happen, via the roles of leading and linking.

- **Leading insiders.** More has been written about leadership than probably all the other roles of managing combined. But here it is seen as one role of managing, not separated from and superior to the rest of it. *Leading* means (a) encouraging and developing individuals to function more effectively, (b) building and maintaining teams, and (c) establishing and strengthening culture and community that bind all the people of the unit together.

- **Linking to outsiders.** Research has demonstrated time and again that managers are external linkers as much as they are internal leaders.[29] In this role, managers (a) build up networks of outside contacts, (b) serve as figureheads, to represent their unit externally, (c) convey influence outward, to champion the needs of their unit and lobby for its causes, and (d) transmit outside influence back into the unit, judiciously.

Managing on the Action Plane

Managers also manage action, *almost* directly. When we hear that "Mary-Anne is a doer," we don't usually mean that she does the operating work—makes the products or maintains the machines, for example. Rather, one step removed on the action plane, managers help other people get things done. They champion changes, join projects, handle disturbances, do deals. Described below are the roles of doing on the inside and dealing on the outside.

- **Doing on the inside.** Managers handle disturbances reactively as well as manage opportunities proactively, the latter, for example, by joining a team, not just to get informed but also to influence its outcome.

- **Dealing on the outside**. Dealing is the other side of doing, its external manifestation. Managers do deals with outsiders, including suppliers, funders, and partners, also with other managers within their own organization. They also use their external networks to conduct negotiations, for example, with partners in joint ventures and unions that represent the workers.

Now we can appreciate the dangers of overemphasizing one role of managing: it could lead to the lopsided practice of managing (in the shape of Figure 3.6). Like an unbalanced wheel at resonant frequency, the job risks oscillating out of control. This is one job that must remain well-rounded. Thinking is heavy (too much of it can weigh a manager down), while acting is light (too much of that and the manager can fly off in all directions). An overemphasis on leading can distract managers from the content of managing, while an overemphasis on linking can reduce the job to public relations. The manager who only communicates never gets anything done, while the manager who has to *do* most everything ends up doing it all alone.

So, how to stay well-rounded? By facing a whole set of conundrums that are integral to managerial work (see box).

Having re-viewed the parts and players of the organization, and having considered the art, craft, and science of decision making, strategy formation, and managerial work, we turn now to the basic building blocks of organization design.

THE INESCAPABLE CONUNDRUMS OF MANAGING

To appreciate the true complexities of managing, please consider these conundrums. A *conundrum* is some problem that cannot be resolved, although it can be alleviated. Here are eight[30]:

1. **The predicament of planning.** This is perhaps the most basic of all the conundrums, the plague of every manager. **How to plan, strategize, just plain think, let alone think ahead, in such a hectic job?** Put differently, how to get in deep when there is so much pressure to get it done?

2. **The quandary of connecting. How to keep informed—in contact, "in touch"—when managing by its very nature is removed from the very thing being managed?** Yesterday you were writing articles, today you are managing a bunch of professors writing articles.

3. **The labyrinth of decomposition.** The world of organizations is chopped into little pieces—departments and divisions, products and services, programs and budgets. Managers are supposed to oversee and integrate this whole confusing affair. **Where to find synthesis in a world so decomposed by analysis?**

4. **The mysteries of measuring.** Many of the most important things to be managed, such as culture and management itself, don't lend themselves to easy measurement. Hence, **how to manage what you can't rely on measuring?**

5. **The dilemma of delegating.** Managers who are connected receive a great deal of information, much of it informal—opinion, hearsay, even gossip. Thus, **how is the manager to delegate when so much of their information is personal, oral, and often privileged?**

6. **The ambiguity of acting.** When a manager delays deciding, to better understand a situation, everyone else can be held back from acting. But the manager who leaps to action can be no better. **How to act decisively in a complicated, nuanced world,** somewhere between paralysis by analysis and extinction by instinct?[31]

7. **The riddle of change.** Constant change can be as dysfunctional as no change. **How to manage change when there is the need to maintain continuity?**

8. **The clutch of confidence.** Management requires confidence: who wants to be managed by someone afraid to act, any more than by

someone who always acts fearlessly. Hence, **how to maintain a sufficient level of confidence without crossing over into arrogance?**

How can any manager possibly deal with all these conundrums concurrently? To repeat, by facing them, to alleviate their effects. These conundrums are not distractions; they *are* managing! Thus, **to manage is to be walking through a multidimensional space on all kinds of tightropes. Managers have to get the balance right, a dynamic balance.**

PART II

THE BUILDING BLOCKS OF ORGANIZATION DESIGN

Let's get back to that cow, introduced in Chapter 2. The parts of this living beast can easily be identified. But unless you are hungry for a steak, or are a veterinarian who has to fix one of these parts, whole cows are more interesting than parts of cows. While we may not design cows, we do design organizations, as well as fix them, and for this we need to understand their basic building blocks.

Here, hence, we shall have to decompose the design of organizations in order to recompose whole organizations. So please bear with me in the three chapters that follow, on the mechanisms of coordination, the elements of design, and the contextual factors that drive these parameters one way or another. I have tried to keep these as short as necessary, to focus the rest of the book on whole organizations. (Please do read Chapter 4, but if you scan the **bold face** sentences of Chapters 5 and 6, I won't tell anybody.)

CHAPTER 4

The Mechanisms to Coordinate

To make a movie or score a goal, people doing different things have to work together. This is called *coordination*, and it is the essence of organizing, following the *division of labor*.

The division of labor is pretty straightforward, dictated by the mission of the organization and the technology it uses. To make a film, you need writers, actors, camera crew, directors, and so on. To play hockey, you need forwards, defense, a goalie, and coaches to guide them. Each player in a film or a game knows what to do, but to put all their work together—to *coordinate* it—is another matter. However naturally this happens in a cow, nature fails us when it comes to coordinating a herd of cows, let alone a herd of filmmakers.

A barking dog may help for the cows, but you have to be careful about a barking director on a film set, even if sometimes necessary. This is a form of *direct supervision*, one of the six coordinating mechanism described in this chapter. Another is *mutual adjustment,* as when the actors on the set discuss how to play a particular scene. The other four are forms of *standardization*: of the *work* itself (such as specifying how the extras should walk across a scene in the film), of the *outputs* of the work (establishing a budget to make the film for less than $300 million), of the *skills* brought to the work (hiring actors trained at Juilliard), and of the *norms* that influence the work (making the film to celebrate beavers and bears).

Mutual Adjustment: Communicating Directly

Using mutual adjustment, people coordinate directly, through conversation or otherwise, web-like.  We find this both where work is simple and where it is complex: two people running the rapids in a canoe or dozens of them developing a new technology. The two in the canoe have to react to each other's movements. The one in the back sets the course, while the one in the front makes the quick move to avoid hitting a rock head-on, whereafter the other has to straighten out the canoe before it hits that rock sideways. Much the same happens as hockey players take the puck down the ice, responding to each other's movements, and in offices where managers have to adapt to unexpected events quickly— like that rock in the rapids. Even bees do it:

> Scout bees...fly out from the bivouac in all directions in the search for a new permanent nest site. When a suitable site is found...the scouts return and signal the direction and distance of the find.... Different scouts may announce different sites simultaneously and a contest ensues. Finally the site being advertised most vigorously by the largest number of workers wins, and the entire swarm flies off to it.[32]

Coordination and control are two different concepts. *Mutual adjustment* is coordination without control, while the other four coordinating mechanisms are different forms of control.

Direct Supervision: Issuing Instructions

Put eight rowers into a racing shell and mutual adjustment no longer works. They have to take orders from the coxswain, who calls the stroke. Not exactly a barking boss, but direct supervision nonetheless.

More commonly, **direct supervision comes from a manager who, at the center of a hub, can grasp the whole of a situation in his or her head, and thus coordinate the work of others by informing them what to do.** In football, the quarterback 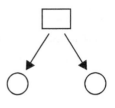 (or coach) calls the play for the whole offensive team, and the players coordinate accordingly.

Both mutual adjustment and direct supervision are informal, flexible mechanisms of coordination. They function in real time, whether across several people or executed by a single individual. In contrast, the four mechanisms of standardization that follow are usually built into the formal structure of the organization, many pre-programmed by analysts in its technostructure—hence they constitute coordination by design.[33]

Standardizing the Work: Establishing Rules

Once that play is called in football, everyone snaps into action according to the programmed design. (The quarterback calls #6, so the fullback takes the ball up the middle.) Much the same thing happens in an automobile assembly plant: everyone is posi- 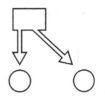 tioned in the chain to install some part in a specified way.

Standardization of the work can take the form of job specifications—that specify exactly how to do the work, as Frederick Taylor did with workers a century ago, and as IKEA does with us today when we follow its instructions to assemble a piece of furniture at home. In organizations, this usually applies to the operators who do rather unskilled work, but it can also take the form of general rules that apply to everyone, as in a dress code.

Organizations that are rule-bound, with most of their operating work standardized, are known as *bureaucracies.* This is how the word was used initially, although it has since taken on a pejorative meaning (as we shall discuss later). But would you fly in an airplane that is not rule-bound, say, with the pilots chatting about how they feel like landing the plane today?

Standardizing the Outputs: Controlling Performance

If the work itself cannot be standardized, sometimes the outputs or results of it can be. When I get into a taxi, for instance, I don't normally give orders, like "speed up," or "hit the brakes." Instead, I standardize the results,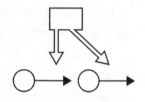
the target: "Please take me to 7 rue Sept." Likewise, a worker may be told, not how to drill a hole, but to make it 7 centimeters in diameter so that it will fit with a round peg made by another worker. And in much the same way, the manager of a division in a corporation may be given a standard such as to cut costs by 10 percent. Much of this kind of standardizing is done by analysts, with titles such as *planner*, *controller*, and *quality control engineer*.

Standardizing the Skills and Knowledge: Prior Training

Training is a way to coordinate work that can be repetitive but is highly skilled. A team of surgeons and nurses can perform open-heart surgery without a word being said or an in-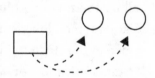
struction being given. They coordinate thanks to the standardization of their skills and knowledge to the point where each person knows exactly what to expect of the others (unless something goes wrong, in which case it's time for mutual adjustment!). They are like stage actors who may appear to be impromptu, but in fact have learned their lines well.

Here, in effect, people work as a set—together yet apart—just like baseball players who coordinate perfectly for that double play. It's all pre-set, in the training. In other words, **extensive training** standardizes people's skills and knowledge, thus enabling them to coordinate almost automatically.

Standardizing the Norms: Sharing Beliefs

"Love God and do what you like," say the Jesuits.[34] They say this because they know full well that if their recruits love God the way the Jesuits want them to, they will do what the Order likes. And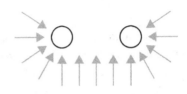
vigorously—for the common cause. **Standardized norms (or values) commit people to common beliefs that enable them to coordinate with each other.**[35] Whereas the standards of work and outputs are imposed, and the standards of skills are learned, the standards of norms are imbibed, often through processes of indoctrination, as well as socialization. Hence, they go much deeper, beyond people's activities, to their souls, so to speak. Strongly established norms can sometimes explain why some organizations function so well—say, a soccer-football team that comes out of nowhere to win the Premier League title in England.

We can better understand these forms of standardization by comparing them with their opposite, customization, which relies more on mutual adjustment and direct supervision for coordination. The box presents a continuum of this, from one extreme to the other.

CUSTOMIZATION BEYOND STANDARDIZATION

The opposite of standardization is customization: everything is different instead of everything being the same.[36] Compare the kids' art on a wall at home with the black screen of the TV nearby. The continuum below shows various degrees of standardization and customization.

Pure Standardization	Segmented Standardization	Customized Standardization	Tailored Customization	Pure Customization

- At one extreme is *pure standardization*, this book in print, for example: take it or leave it as is.

- In *segmented standardization,* you can choose from among a number of standardized options. Besides the print version of this book, you can get it in e-form, audio, even braille. While most everything is standardized these days, often that is in segmented form (e.g., you can get table salt from the sea or a mine, in white or pink, also kosher).
- At the other extreme is *pure customization*—say, an architecturally designed house that has been totally built to your specifications, or a great feature film—both unlike any other.
- Next to this is *tailored customization*—a standard offering tailored to your particular needs. Just as padding is added on your right, drooping shoulder to the suit you buy off the rack, so the cardiac surgeon selects the stent that best fits your artery.
- And in the middle of all this is *customized standardization.* You assemble what you like from an offering of standardized components. You put together your university degree from the courses that are offered in the syllabus; you make up your own meal from the given offerings on the buffet table.

All of the Above

While many organizations favor one of the mechanisms of coordination, few can get by without using several, usually all. The standardization of work may dominate an automobile assembly plant, but sometimes the foreman gives orders to the workers. In football, the quarterback may call the play, yet the players execute it in rather standardized fashion, based on a certain level of training. And should the ball be fumbled, watch for mutual adjustment as a player on the other team picks it up and runs, with the improvised blocking of his teammates. That they do so with great energy suggests that standardized norms are at play here too.

Just how fundamental are these six coordinating mechanisms is suggested both by how far back they go, and that so many famous writers in management have focused on one or another of them.

Before anyone ever thought about management, tribes of Homo

sapiens presumably coordinated by mutual adjustment, with some direct supervision from the strongest member. As we became more civilized, so to speak, with the appearance of chiefs, then lords and monarchs and so on, direct supervision became prominent. This carried straight into the twentieth century, when the first writings on management focused on control by formal authority—namely, direct supervision.[37]

While this continued, in came standardization, on various fronts: Frederick Taylor's scientific management (1911) to standardize work on the floors of mines and factories; Peter Drucker's *management by objectives* (1954) to standardize outputs in the managerial offices; and Richard Pascale and Anthony Athos's *The Art of Japanese Management* (1982) that attributed the enormous success of Japanese companies postwar to their engaging cultures, namely the standardization of their norms.[38] Meanwhile, the rise of professionalism through the twentieth century introduced the standardization of skills in many organizations, although as a mechanism of coordination, this has not received equivalent attention in the management literature. Currently, the literature of management gives considerable attention to teams, task forces, and networks, all manifestations of mutual adjustment.

This closes the loop of our coordinating mechanisms, from the tribes of our ancestors to the technologies of our times.

CHAPTER 5

The Elements of Design

This chapter introduces the elements of design, the knobs that can be turned to structure an organization. We start this description from the ground up, with the design of positions (the cells of the organization's body): their scope, degree of formalization, and the training and indoctrination they require. Next comes the design of the superstructure (the skeleton of the organization): how these positions are grouped into units, what size these units should be, and how much decision-making power should be decentralized to them. Finally, there is the fleshing out of the superstructure: the systems of planning and control and the lateral linkages to connect all these positions and units together.

Designing Positions: Scope

Positions can be narrow or broad, specialized or general. The pitcher in baseball is highly specialized—in the American League, they don't even bat—whereas in cricket, many players "bowl" and all of them bat. In his 1776 book *The Wealth of Nations*, Adam Smith described what has become the most famous example of extensive specialization of labor—in the manufacture of pins.

One man draws out the wire, another straightens it, a third cuts it, a fourth points it, a fifth grinds it at the top for receiving the head; to make the head requires two or three distinct operations; to put it on is a peculiar business, to whiten the pins is another; it is even a trade by itself to put them into the paper.[39]

Why so hyperspecialized? Because it is efficient. Smith noted that in one pin factory, ten men specialized in their work were able to turn out about forty-eight hundred pins per day, whereas if one had to do all this, the result might not even have been twenty.

Many people don't relish having narrow jobs. Hence, two centuries after Smith came *job enlargement,* as in a call center that redesigns the operators' jobs so that each can address a variety of customer questions instead of being limited to pat answers for a few of them (more about this in Chapter 8).

Designing Positions: Formalization

Organizations formalize work to proscribe discretion in carrying it out, ultimately to predict and control it, whether by specifying the work directly, attaching specifications to the workflow, or establishing rules to control the work across the whole organization.

As the author of this book, my work is minimally formalized: I have considerable control over what I write and how, subject to the rules of proper grammar, of course. But the work of the printers of this book is highly formalized. First, job descriptions specify exactly what each worker does. Second, along with their work comes a docket that specifies the size of the pages, the paper to be used, the binding to put on, and so forth. And third, workers in printing plants usually have to follow a lot more rules than do university professors—for example, when to start work and how much time is allotted for lunch.

If you believe that the pin-making kind of work is gone today, try flipping hamburgers at a fast-food chain. However, if you think that the work of professors and physicians is not otherwise formalized, consider all the rules that are promulgated by their professional associations.

Designing Positions: Training and Indoctrination

Here organization design specifies what skills and knowledge need to be brought to the job as well as what norms have to be assimilated there. You can get a job at McDonald's and be flipping hamburgers in no time. But don't try to walk into a hospital and expect to do surgery right away. **One job is *unskilled*, the other, being skilled, requires extensive *professional* education, followed by considerable on-the-job training.** Here is a list of training requirements for some jobs in a retail store: working in a warehouse (on the job); checker (one week at a training center); meat cutter (six weeks, part school, part on the job); butcher (normally two years on the job); and store manager (normally two years on the job, with an occasional week in school).

When an organization hires professionals, it surrenders a good deal of control over these people to the external institutions that have trained them—in other words, that have standardized their skills and knowledge—and to the professional associations that continue to upgrade and enforce these standards. Think of the protocols in medicine and the principles in accounting. Here is where we find true "communities of practice."

In between skilled and unskilled work is that of *craft*: not formally trained so much as extensively apprenticed on the job, under the supervision of an expert. Thus, while there are schools for chefs, many of them learn by working under an experienced chef. Likewise, "professional" athletes are generally trained by their coaches.

Organizations that have unique cultures tend to be especially concerned that their people assimilate the culture and internalize the norms. Hence, they are inclined to develop customized programs, in house, to *indoctrinate* their people, or, if you prefer a less loaded word, *socialize* them. Think of an army with its boot camp or a company that rotates new hires so they get a sense of the whole place. Of course, some indoctrination is usually built into the professional training too, as when, besides courses such as anatomy, medical students are taught how to behave like proper physicians.

Designing the Superstructure: Grouping into Units

Here we come to the skeleton of the organization, the bones that hold its parts together. We consider how the positions are grouped into formal units, and how these units are grouped into successively larger ones to form the hierarchy of authority, also how large these different units should be.

Grouping gets so much attention that it has come to be seen as almost synonymous with structuring—hence the obsession with those organization charts. Well, just as there is a lot more to our bodies than our skeletons, so too there is a lot more to our organizations than grouping, even though they can no more exist without such grouping than we can exist without our skeletons.

Why Group?

We group for three reasons:

- *To encourage mutual adjustment.* By being grouped together, not only physically but also administratively, people are encouraged to communicate and cooperate. For example, a law firm may designate a specialized unit for those lawyers engaged in family practice, to encourage them to share their experience.

- *To enable direct supervision.* Even specialized physicians who work largely on their own need a chief—for example, to take the lead in hiring new people and to help resolve conflicts among them. Usually the manager can best hold things together in a unit.

- *To attain a common result.* The retail branch of a bank might put its agents selling insurance, brokerage, and trust services in the same unit to encourage more cross-selling.

Of course, encouraging all this within a unit can discourage it across units. Will those family practice lawyers be inclined to seek out their colleagues in corporate law when they need their advice? See the box about silos and slabs in organizations.

SILOS AND SLABS IN ORGANIZATIONS

We all know about silos, those vertical cylinders that keep grain from spilling all over the farms. Organizations have silos too—those units we are discussing here. When you look at an organization chart, does it strike you as being designed to encourage 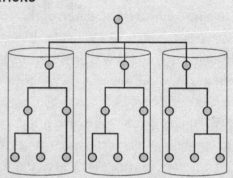 people to communicate across the units, or discourage it? Organizations may need silos for the sake of specialization, but they don't need impenetrable walls. Or to put this another way, reversing another popular metaphor, **it's not seamlessness we need in our organizations but good seams**—tailored connections between the units.

If *silos* **are vertical barriers to the horizontal flow of information in an organization, discouraging lateral mutual adjustment in favor of hierarchical direct supervision, then** *slabs* **are horizontal barriers to the vertical flow of information, from one level in the hierarchy to another**—for example, between the salespeople and the sales manager, or the sales VP and the CEO. This problem is exacerbated when these different levels of the hierarchy are placed, quite literally, on the different floors of the building (e.g., all the VPs on one floor)—because people seem more inclined to walk horizontally than go up and down vertically. (Here we have slabs made of concrete!)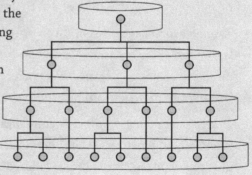

Thus a CEO on the top floor is as far as a person can get from what is happening on the ground.

Maybe it will become easier to cut across all these silos and slabs when we realize that they are just figments of our lack of imagination. Kao, a Japanese manufacture of personal care and other products, developed a reputation for running its meetings in open spaces, and allowing anyone passing by to join in—a worker in an executive committee, a CEO in a factory meeting.

How to Group?

On what basis should positions be grouped into units and these units into larger ones? **Here are several common bases for doing this**:

- **By *what* they do**. The offensive squad in football scores, the defensive squad stops the other team from scoring. Manufacturing companies often group their workers by the different *functions* they perform, such as purchasing, production, marketing, and sales.

- **By *how* they do it**. The internists prescribe, the surgeons cut. The violinists play the strings; the brass play the horns.

- **By *why* they do it,** namely to achieve a common result. A diversified company assigns its laptop business to one unit, printers to another, customer service for both to a third.

- **By *where* they do it**. Miners work underground, dentists work on teeth, drinks are served at the bar, sales are made in Saskatchewan.

- **By *for whom* they do it**. Pediatricians do it for children, geriatricians do it for their grandparents.

- **By *when* they do it**. A factory has a day shift and a night shift.

Of course, these categories can overlap. Gynecologists, for example, are grouped not only by whom they treat but also by how they do so, even where they do so.

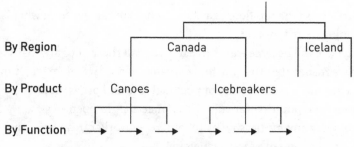

FIGURE 5.1 Stacking the Bases of Grouping

Some of these bases of grouping fall into two broad categories: by *means* (what and how) and by *ends* (why and for whom). Grouping by means favors specialization, so that people can learn from each other, but at the expense of coordination with other specialists. Grouping by ends does the opposite: it encourages coordination across the workflow but at the expense of specialization within it.

An important message in all this is that **there is no magic formula for grouping positions and units, just a number of options that trade off one set of advantages for another.** This means that some consultant can always find a better way to structure, which can also prove to be worse. Hence, here we have the motto of too many organizations: when in doubt, *reorganize!* Better still, *de-layer*—that is, delete a slab or two of those costly managers. Unfortunately, or should I say fortunately, **grouping is no panacea for organization design, just one design element among many.**

In one sense, however, organizations can have their grouping cake and eat it too. They can structure the way a campfire is built, by stacking the slabs first one way and then another. A manufacturing company can group by business function at the base, then by product line, finally by region (Figure 5.1).

Designing the Superstructure: Sizing the Units

How many angels can dance on the head of a pin? In the Middle Ages, theologians were mocked about asking such questions. Now the question is: how many positions can be grouped under the heels of a manager? And the answer is...five, or six. So claimed the classic management theorist Lyndall Urwick: "No supervisor can supervise directly the work of more than five or, at the most, six subordinates whose work interlocks."[40]

Well, then, why do one hundred of us at the McGill Faculty of Management whose work interlocks (to create bachelors, masters, and doctoral degrees) report to one dean, or that many workers in a factory to one foreman, or a like number of musicians to a conductor, whereas if you try to play hockey with a line of four forwards instead of three, you may lose the game because of a weakened defense? Must every one of these units be brought down, or rounded up, to five or six members? Obviously not. I imagine that Urwick had in mind VPs reporting to a CEO. But think of all the other arrangements that exist in organizations, indeed sometimes even in the case of those VPs. Enough of generalizing out of context.

The label is the problem. **We commonly call this design element** *span of control*, **as if it's all about control by a manager—namely, coordination by direct supervision. It is not.** *Size of unit* **is a better label, because other mechanisms of coordination come into play here.** All those professors and workers and musicians can report to a single manager because their work is largely controlled by some form of standardization, not direct supervision.

In contrast, the small number of players on a forward line in hockey is explained by their reliance on mutual adjustment for coordination—convenient, frequent, informal communication. The greater the need for this, the *smaller* the unit has to be. Dozens of people in a unit can hardly communicate casually. (So go explain how lacrosse, similar in some ways to hockey, was played by up to a thousand indigenous Americans.) Hence, while a hundred professors reporting to a dean can be fine when it comes to teaching courses (with "area coordinators," who are not managers, overseeing who teaches what), six can be too many when it comes to doing research in teams. And bear in mind that although such teams may designate a manager (although hockey lines do not), the work of that person may be more about linking the team out—for example, serving as its spokesperson—than leading it in.

Designing the Superstructure: Untangling Decentralization

After a century of discussion about the terms *centralization* and *decentralization* in the management literature, they remain as confusing as ever. But **what else can we expect from the label *de*-centralization, as if centralization is the default position?**

Consider an automobile company with five business units, one for each model of car that it makes, with the manager of each unit having most of the decision-making power. As we shall discuss at greater length later, General Motors in the 1920s was the famous case of this. Its CEO labeled this "decentralization," in reference to the managers of the Chevrolet, Pontiac, Buick, Oldsmobile, and Cadillac businesses.[41] But can a company that had so many thousands of employees, five of whom held the lion's share of the power, be called *decentralized*? Maybe, compared with a company whose CEO at the headquarters had that power, but otherwise?

When all the power for decision making rests with a single individual, an organization can obviously be called centralized; when that power is dispersed more or less equally among everyone, it can obviously be called decentralized. On one side is an autocratic regime in government, on the other, a traditional kibbutz in Israel where the members share most everything (more on this later). Between these two extremes, however, is where decentralization gets interesting.

Decision-making power can be *delegated vertically,* down the hierarchy, more or less, or it can be *dispersed horizontally,* to nonmanagers, whether analysts, support staffers, or operators at the base. And this power can go *partially* or *comprehensively,* for example, for hiring decisions only, or else for most of the decisions pertaining to a unit.

With this is mind, we can consider various versions of decentralization. The decentralization just described at General Motors was vertical and comprehensive, but seemingly limited to the managers of the five divisions. When staff analysts have power over, say, the budgets that control the spending of everyone else, this can be described as decentralization that is horizontal, selective, and also limited. Alternatively, when professionals in the operating core control many of the decisions that affect them—physicians in hospitals, for example— this can be described as comprehensive horizontal decentralization.

Considering the coordinating mechanism in these terms, direct supervision is the most horizontally centralizing whereas mutual adjustment is the least, with the forms of standardization—first of the work, then of the outputs, next of the skills, and finally of the norms—falling in between, in that order.

Fleshing Out the Superstructure: Systems of Planning and Control

Once positions have been established and grouped into units, with their size and decisional power determined, there remains the need to put some flesh on these bones and flow all this together, as do the nerves of our bodies. **Systems of planning and control coordinate by standardizing outputs across positions and units; liaison devices coordinate by encouraging mutual adjustment.**

You are organizing COP77 in 2077, to deal with climate change... finally. There's an awful lot to do, so you lay it all out on a spreadsheet, as a set of *action plans*: to choose the speakers, choreograph the events, cater the coffee breaks, coddle the lobbyists. You will establish one or more units to do each and decentralize considerable power to them to get it done. But for each unit, you need to establish *performance controls* of various kinds: schedules to meet, budgets to spend, and so on.

Action plans delineate intended targets, or outputs—what is to be achieved and when, but not how—while performance controls

measure how successfully these targets have been met. Action planning is essentially top down, beginning, in theory at least (later we shall discuss practice), with the *formulation* of strategies by the senior management, which are deconstructed into specific projects, programs, budgets, schedules, and other operating plans for *imple-mentation* by everyone else. Performance controls measure the after-the-fact results of these actions, from the bottom up the hierarchy (although these controls are usually designed near the top of it, by the analytical staff who report to the senior management).

For a graphic example of how targets can influence the way people behave, consider how scoring is tabulated in hockey. The player who scores a goal gets a point. But so too does the player who passed the puck to that scorer, and even the one who passed the puck to that passer. These are called *assists*, and they count for as much as goals. How's that for encouraging teamwork? Compare this with singling out the CEO's remuneration in a corporation, based on increases in its share price. How's that for encouraging narcissism?

Fleshing Out the Superstructure: Lateral Linkages

All the design elements so far discussed can take structural design only so far, because **much that matters in organizations requires** *lateral linkages* **of a less formal nature, to encourage mutual adjustment across the silos and the slabs.** A whole set of these have found increasing application in recent times.

Most simple are *liaison positions*, designated to sit between two units and connect them together. A purchasing engineer can link engineering with purchasing, to keep the cost of components down. These positions have no formal authority, just the responsibility to find ways to get the two sides to cooperate.

Integrating managers take this a step further, by having some formal authority, for instance, over the resources available to the units. Thus a brand manager in a consumer-goods firm, responsible for a particular product, can use control of its budget to negotiate with engineering to design the product and manufacturing to produce it.

Meetings, standing committees, teams, and *task forces* also foster mutual adjustment. We know about meetings, which bring people together to discuss common issues, share information, and perhaps make joint decisions. Think about all such meetings needed to organize that COP77. Plus many meetings are impromptu: people just bump into each other, and discuss what's on their minds. Other meetings are scheduled on an ad hoc basis—one time only—or else regularly, perhaps with designated membership, in which case they become *standing committees*, as part of the formal structure. Such a committee for COP77 might bring together, every Tuesday at 9 a.m., representatives of the teams that are dealing with various aspects of the event.

The board of directors of an organization is, in effect, a standing committee, with regular meetings to review its overall performance. Even the players of a hockey team can be thought to constitute a standing committee when they meet in the dressing room between periods to review the game so far.

These days, of course, many meetings take place virtually, over the internet. This may seem less formal, but it can be as orchestrated as a concert. Instead of a baton, the conductor has a mute button. Moreover, on Zoom people don't bump into each other at the coffee machine. Where's the key to press for serendipity? How to click for spontaneity? This wonderful technology can wreak havoc upon mutual adjustment.

A team or task force brings a group of people together temporarily, to accomplish a particular *project*—say, to develop a product or restructure an organization—and then disband, at which point the members return to their home units. A research team in a university might bring together professors from geography, geology, and geophysics to test some new theory.

A team can, of course, also bring in members from outside the organization—say, in this last example, a geologist from a mining company—or even be made up of people from various organizations, as is common in filmmaking, which makes substantial use of independent freelancers. A *joint venture* brings together people from two or more organizations in a partnership—for example, to develop a new airplane. (In Chapter 20, we discuss "Organizations Outward Bound," namely, the propensity in recent years to break down the traditional boundaries of organizations in these and other ways.)

Matrix Structure

Earlier we discussed stacking up different levels of grouping in an organization the way campfire logs are stacked one way and then another, because a single one cannot provide all the coordination that is necessary. Further to this, a line and staff structure can help, as can the lateral linkages just discussed. But further steps may be necessary to enhance collaboration, especially across the silos. This is when organizations turn to *matrix structure*. It encourages collaboration by violating one of the sacred principles of management, called *unity of command*, which means that everyone must report to a single boss. **In matrix structure, people report to two or more bosses, which increases ambiguity for the sake of collaboration.**

A matrix structure may be permanently built into the superstructure or else set up temporarily to execute a project. As an example of the former, those purchasing engineers discussed earlier can report to both the manager of purchasing or the manager of engineering, to help bridge the gap between the two units. Likewise, a regional sales team can report to both the VP of sales and the VP of the region. The organization lives with the ambiguity in order to sustain a balance of power. As an example of a temporary matrix, consider a team of designers, engineers, and marketers working together on a project to develop a new product. Each may report to both the manager of the project and the manager of their functional home unit.

Such matrix arrangements are more common than you might think, even if not by that name. After all, **most of us have been raised in a matrix structure called a family. Ambiguity of authority is a fact**

of life there, so why not in our organizations? Resolving conflicts through informal negotiations among equals, rather than having to rely on the formal power of a "superior" over "subordinates" sounds pretty grown-up to me!

To summarize, all these lateral linkages can be seen along a continuum, with pure functional structure (grouped by means) at one end and pure market structure (grouped by ends) at the other, while the liaison positions, integrating managers, meetings, teams, task forces, and standing committees fall in between, and matrix structures in the middle.[42] Add all this up and you can appreciate why in recent years there has been such a proliferation of people with "manager" in their titles.

CHAPTER 6

Design in Context

The original version of this book identified a set of conditions—called *contingency*, or *situational*, *factors*—that drive the design elements to take one shape or another.[43] These include the age and size of the organization, the technical system used in its operations, the complexity, dynamism, and hostility of its external environment, and the power relationships that pervade it. The following propositions describe these relationships.

Age and Size

The *age* of an organization and its *size* play key roles in the design of its structure.

- **The older an organization, the more formalized its behavior.** As an organization ages, it tends to repeat its behaviors, which thus become more predictable and therefore more amenable to formalization.

- **The larger an organization, the more formalized its behavior.** Just as the older organization formalizes what it has seen before, so the larger organization formalizes what it sees often. "Listen,

I've heard that story five times today. Just fill in the form like it says."

- **The larger an organization, the more elaborate its structure, that is, the more specialized its positions and units and the more developed its administration.** With greater size comes more specialization. Only a large barber shop can have a specialist to cut children's hair. And with greater specialization of the positions comes more *differentiation* of the units, therefore more elaboration of the hierarchy. In a small barber shop the barber greets you, cuts your hair, takes your money, and says goodbye. In the large one, different people may do each of these tasks.

- **Structure reflects the age of the industry.** This is a curious finding, but one that, we shall see, holds up rather well. No matter what its own age, the structure of an organization can reflect the age of its industry. In other words, even new organizations in an industry may be structured more or less like the older ones. As we shall see, industries that have been around for some time, such as banking and hotels, tend to rely on structures that are rather formalized, compared with the more recent high-tech industries that tend to rely on looser, more organic structures.

Technical System

Technical system refers to the instruments used in the operations to produce the outputs. This should be distinguished from *technology*, which refers to the body of knowledge that may be used to design such a system. Mass production is a technical system, information science, a technology.

- **The more the technical system controls the work of the operators, the more formalized is, not only their operating work, but also the administrative structure of the organization.** In other words, expect more structured relationships in the headquarters of an automobile company, where the operating work is rather controlled, than in a film company, where the operating people have far more discretion. In one, the propensity to control spills over from the operations into the administration; in the other, it is the casual nature of relationships that spills over. (More on this in Chapter 17, about *contamination*.)

- **The more complex the technical system, the more elaborate, expert, and influential the support staff**. Organizations that use complex machinery require staff experts to design or select it as well as to maintain and modify it. The next proposition elaborates on this one.

- **The automation of the operating core transforms a bureau-cratic administrative structure into an organic one**. Here, again, we have a curious proposition: As the operating work be-comes structured to the point of being automated, the rest of the organization loosens up! Machines are obedient: they don't need to be controlled by technocratic standards. So out go the analysts who served as the "maintenance crew for the human machinery," as Braverman has described the human resource staff.[44] And in come support specialists to work more flexibly in teams to deal with the real machinery. While a nonautomated assembly line is replete with workers doing boring things, a fully automated one is overseen by specialists doing interesting things.

Environment

Environment refers to the conditions that surround an organization.

- **The more dynamic an organization's environment, the more organic its structure**. It stands to reason that organizations in stable environments, where their people know what to expect, can rely on standardization for coordination. But when external conditions become dynamic—unexpected competition arises, the economy falls into recession—organizations have to be far more flexible, through the use of direct supervision and mutual adjustment for coordination. Armies may march in peacetime, but that doesn't do much good when they are engaged in guerrilla warfare.

- **The more complex an organization's environment, the more decentralized its structure.** An organization can be rather centralized when much of the information needed to make decisions can be understood in one place. But when the necessary information is widespread and complicated, power has to be diffused to whoever has the knowledge to deal with it. Note that a simple environment can be dynamic (e.g., the manufacturer of dresses may not be able to predict style from one session to the next), just as a complex one can be stable (e.g., open-heart surgery uses complicated equipment but is normally rather predictable).

Power

Power, too, is a factor in organization design.

- **The greater the external control of an organization, the more centralized and formalized its structure.** This important proposition indicates that external influencers with considerable power over an organization tend to drive it toward a bureaucratic structure. That is because they are inclined to exercise that power by imposing extensive performance measures on the organization, and holding its central management responsible for attaining that performance.[45] Stock market analysts fixate on upping the share price of companies, and some governments measure galore in the schools that they fund. This makes these organizations easier to control from the outside, no matter how much damage it can sometimes cause inside (more on this later). Moreover, the chief of an organization that is externally controlled has to be especially careful about its actions, hence may be inclined to proliferate rules to avoid being embarrassed by the actions of its people.

- **Power divided between pockets of external influencers of an organization can breed conflict within the organization.** In other words, power divisions outside tend to get mirrored inside, as each side lines up its own internal supporters. For example, some experts believe that prisons should exist to rehabilitate their inmates, while people in the local community may be more concerned about ensuring custody. Each may lobby managers of the prison sympathetic to their concerns, thus fomenting conflict within the administration of the prison.

- **Fashion also plays a role in the structuring of organizations.** Ideally, the design elements are chosen according to the dictates of age, size, technical system, and environment. In fact, however, many organizations are drawn to structures that are currently fashionable, even when they may be inappropriate. Just as Paris has its salons of haute couture, so New York has its offices of "haute structure," those consulting firms that promote the currently "hot" technique to all their clients. And have you ever seen an article in a business magazine that qualifies its pitch for the latest technique with "WARNING: Not to be used in hospitals!" or whatever. Likewise, while every kind of structure can be found in every country, national culture may create a bias toward certain ones—perhaps more formalization in Swiss organizations, less in Italian ones.

This completes Part II of the book, having categorized, every which way, the blocks that we need to build our organization structures. This analysis has been a necessary step toward the synthesis that follows.

PART III

FOUR FUNDAMENTAL FORMS OF ORGANIZATION

The time has come to put the Humpty Dumpty of organizing back together again, or, if you prefer, to return to complete cows. Enough deconstructing the organization into its parts; now we reconstruct these parts into wholes.

If there is no best way to organize, how many ways can there be? Four. To start, at least, in this part of the book. Later we shall consider seven ways, until we will come to the true answer, which is as many ways as we can imagine, under the circumstances. For now, however, we will respect an insight from Yogi Berra, the zany catcher of the New York Yankees baseball team, who, when asked if he would like his pizza cut into four pieces or six, replied: "You'd better make it four, I don't think I can eat six pieces." So, for the sake of your digestion, here are four forms of organizations.

There are times when we need to caricature, or stereotype, reality to sharpen its differences and so better understand it. A limited number of forms can help us do that for organizations. The four discussed in this part of the book—constructed from the blocks that we have been discussing—are labeled personal, programmed, professional, and

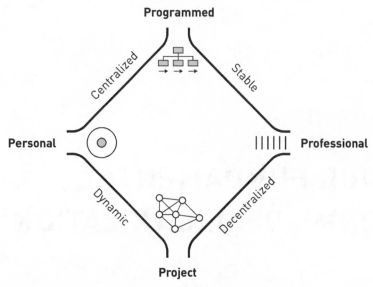

FIGURE III.1 The Four Forms

project. More formally, these are the Personal Enterprise (Chapter 7), Programmed Machine (Chapter 8), Professional Assembly (Chapter 9), and Project Pioneer (Chapter 10), shown in the diamond of Figure III.1.

Think restaurants: a corner diner, a fast-food franchise, a gourmet dining room, a catered event—four very different ways of delivering the same service. One revolves around a single person, the owner; the second is fully programmed; the third relies on the skills of its chefs; and the fourth is customized, as a project. In the natural world, compare a troop of monkeys with the alpha male at its head, a flock of geese flying in formation, ants scurrying around doing their own thing together, and a family of beavers building a dam.

Forms like these are known as *ideal types*—really pure types, since there is nothing ideal about them. Please appreciate that these are not quite reality itself so much as simplifications of reality for the sake of comprehension—although you are likely to find more reality here than you might expect. We will get to the qualifying and the nuancing in due course (Part VI).

CHAPTER 7

The Personal Enterprise

If you want a track team to win the high jump, you find one person who can jump seven feet, not seven people who can each jump one foot.

—Terman's Law of Innovation

Terman's Law of Innovation is true enough—but not if you are running in a relay race. **In the Personal Enterprise, the focus is on the person in charge, the chief.** Think of an entrepreneurial company or a social enterprise run by its founder, a new government department that needs focused management to get established, even a hospital in crisis. Someone may have to take full charge, as the center of a hub from which to exercise direct supervision to get things done.

We shall use a team sport to illustrate each of the forms. Which do you think applies best to the Personal Enterprise, where one person is so influential? Try to think of one before you read on.

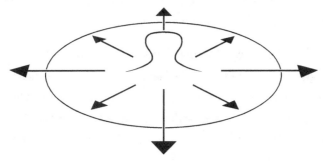

(Logo for the Personal Enterprise)

The answer for this form did not come easily to us—the other three did—but once found, it seems obvious: world cup yacht racing. One person can get the idea, the vision, work with the designer of the hull, engage the crew, and skipper during the races. It's not that the other members of the crew are incidental; it's that their efforts revolve around the chief.

Basic Structure of the Personal Enterprise

The structure of the Personal Enterprise is characterized by what it is not: elaborated. It actually resists structure. In earlier versions of this book, I called it *simple structure*. This form has a loose division of labor and little analytic staff, which means that it avoids the mechanisms of standardization and the systems of planning and control: these are discouraged as a threat to the organization's one authority.

Likewise, there is a limited managerial hierarchy. Instead, the chief tends to have a wide span of control (here the label really applies). In small Personal Enterprises, it is not uncommon for everyone to report to the chief. Hence the logo on the first page of the chapter pictures this form as a flat organization. Often the place does not even have an organization chart—why bother when everyone knows who's boss? A group of my students commented in the study they did of a small manufacturer of pumps: "It is not unusual to see the president of the company engaged in casual conversation with a machine shop mechanic. [That way he is] informed of a machine breakdown even before the shop superintendent is advised." Even in this great big corporation

[Steve] Jobs did not organize [the huge Apple company] into semiautonomous divisions; he closely controlled all of his teams and pushed them to work as one cohesive and flexible company, with one profit and loss bottom line. "We don't have 'divisions' with their own P&L," said Tim Cook, who later succeeded Jobs as CEO. "We run one P&L for the company."[46]

One consequence of all this is that conflict is less likely to arise in these organizations. Any insider who challenges a thin-skinned chief may not last long. And if an outsider—say, a powerful customer—seeks to exert influence, the chief may be inclined to push back, or even take the organization to a less exposed place in the environment.

Like most everything else, decision making and strategy formation tends to revolve around the chief. This can allow for rapid response—if he or she is so inclined. And since such people are oriented to art more than science, look for a good deal of intuition and opportunism in these processes, especially *seeing first* to grab opportunities. Hence the common use here of words like *insight* and *vision*. Accordingly, **the strategy of the Personal Enterprise often reflects the chief's perspective of the world, sometimes even an extrapolation of his or her own personality.**

Conditions and Kinds of Personal Enterprises

Don't look for the Personal Enterprise in an established space agency or a post office, unless it is in crisis. Such organizations need to get beyond simple structures as well as central authority, albeit in different ways. Look for it, instead, for example, in retailing, where one individual may be able to keep control of a chain of many stores, in effect managing them as one store replicated many times. The environment of such retailing, as in other Personal Enterprises, may be simple, but it can also be rather dynamic. With one person calling the shots, the organization can respond quickly.

New organizations, so-called *start-ups*, **typically use this form of organization because a single person has to get them going**—hire the people, establish the facilities, create the culture, set the pace. Hence the *entrepreneurial firm* is the quintessential Personal Enterprise. A strong-willed chief is typically the founder and significantly the owner.

But the Personal Enterprise is hardly restricted to conventional business. Having the same needs are start-ups in government agen-cies, NGOs, and all sorts of *social enterprises* (meaning businesses not owned by investors, sometimes called *not-for-profits*). And, in turn, this personalized kind of leadership is attracted to start-up situations, often to escape the narrow world of bureaucracies.

Once established, however, **so long as the founding chief remains at the helm, the organization may retain this form of structure, especially, but not necessarily, while it remains small**, so that direct supervision can suffice for coordination. Large organizations gener-ally favor a different structure (discussed in Chapter 8). But many business and social enterprises have grown rather large under the tutelage of their founders, to whom everyone continues to turn for guidance, albeit with the other coordinating mechanisms struggling to find their place. Long after its founder's death, someone at Disney told me that the way they continued to make decisions was to ask: "What would Walt have done?"

Crisis is another condition where we can find the Personal Enter-prise. Faced with the need for rapid, consolidated response, again, what better form than that centered on a single individual who calls the shots? In other words, **an established organization in difficulty often reverts to a simple structure to save itself, through what is called *turnaround***. It suspends its established procedures to close ranks around someone who can take charge to clear out the cobwebs, rebuild the culture, refocus the strategy. Sometimes that person is the retired founder himself or herself, as happened some years ago at Apple, Dell, Starbucks, and other start-ups grown large. Entrepre-neurship can be a tough act to follow!

Pros and Cons of the Personal Enterprise

In each of the four forms, we find great strengths as well as debilitat-ing weaknesses, sometimes for the same reason. **No structure can be more dynamic, more engaging, more vibrant than one led by a founder with a vision.** A Personal Enterprise with such leadership can propel itself into a protective niche in its marketplace, to pursue a distinct strategy with determination. No wonder many people jump aboard.

Entrepreneurs can be masters at constructing big pictures from grounded details. As Konusuke Matsushita, founder of renowned Japanese company of his own name (now called Panasonic), put it: "Big things and little things are my job. Middle-level arrangements can be delegated." Of Steve Jobs, Isaacson wrote: "Some leaders push innovations by being good at the big picture. Others do so by mastering details. Jobs did both, relentlessly. As a result, he launched a series of products over three decades that transformed whole industries."[47]

This very strength, however, has brought down many a Personal Enterprise. **Some chiefs get so enmeshed in the details that they lose sight of the big picture.** (Henry Ford said that his customers could have his cars in any color they liked so long as it was black. Black days followed eventually.) **Others get so enamored with the great vision that they lose sight of the details necessary to sustain it.** Think of Steve Jobs, again, in the early years of Apple with his disregard for marketing. "The flipside of his wondrous ability to focus was his fearsome willingness to filter out things he did not wish to deal with.[48] Moreover, the Personal Enterprise is so dependent on one person that should it lose him or her, the whole place can come crashing down.** One heart attack can wipe out the organization's prime mechanism of coordination. Even when the chief remains at the helm but loses interest, the organization can atrophy.

Success can also breed failure in other ways. Many Personal Enterprises are brought down by founders who expanded them at a pace beyond what their markets or finances could handle, thanks either to miscalculation—more likely, lack of calculation—or narcissistic overreach. With great success, the entrepreneurial personality can feel invincible, attributing his or her success to some magical talent, rather than to deep engagement in the business.

Even with sensible growth, to avoid agility metamorphosing into rigidity, the structure may have to develop beyond what the chief is prepared to accept. Together with this comes the challenge of succession in the Personal Enterprise. How to fill the shoes of a chief who has managed in such a personal fashion? Can one entrepreneur succeed another? More likely, the organization may have to metamorphose into another form. Meanwhile, see the box for how not to manage succession.

RUSSIAN ROULETTE WITH FIVE BULLETS

It is striking how many smart entrepreneurs turn to their sons, as if their male progeny must have inherited their talent. Did they inherit that talent from *their* own fathers? There has been some evidence that many entrepreneurs come from families with strong mothers and weak fathers: they grew up being the take-charge types.[49] If so, then their sons grow up under the exact opposite circumstance. I was raised in a vigorous entrepreneurial community, with many of the sons having succeeded their fathers in successful family businesses. Few of these businesses have survived. I concluded that son succession is a game of Russian roulette played with five bullets.

We hear of the occasional story where a son-in-law was the great successor of the founder—for example, Marks & Spencer and Bombardier. Did the daughter marry in the father's image? And how about daughters being the more natural successors of entrepreneurial fathers (especially in families with weak mothers!)? Can this be one great source of succession foregone? If so, and with the more recent rise of female entrepreneurs themselves, maybe *their* sons could make a comeback!

Many people love to work in Personal Enterprises. They relish the intimate, informal relationships, the excitement of growing something new, the charisma of the chief. But others reject all this, feeling like cattle being led to market for someone else's benefit. With the broadening of democratic norms into organizations themselves, the Personal Enterprise has lost some of its luster, perhaps especially among young people entering the workforce—at least as employees, if not founders. To many of them, the Personal Enterprise looks paternalistic or maternalistic, if not downright autocratic.

And this brings us to another place where, unfortunately, we find the Personal Enterprise on the rise at the time of this writing: autocratic government, whether rule by fiat in a nation-state after a coup or the election of a power-obsessed populist.

Has this personal form of organization become an anachronism? Let's hope so in the case of the populist leader, but not elsewhere. Just look at all the exciting start-ups in so many unexpected places, with many young people keen to make a go of something new. **It is the Personal Enterprise, social as well as business, that sustains healthy development in our world of organizations, and it always will.** Thus we must continue to prize this form of organization, not only for creating enterprises and turning established ones around, but also for managing many simple organizations, especially small ones.

CHAPTER 8

The Programmed Machine

In the automobile business, uncertainty is the biggest enemy.

—Thomas Murphy, CEO of General Motors[50]

Now for something completely different, from the simplest structure to the most elaborate (but not the most complex). The logo of the original version of this book is used for the Programmed Machine because, as noted in Chapter 2, it portrays the conventional, hierarchical view of the organization.

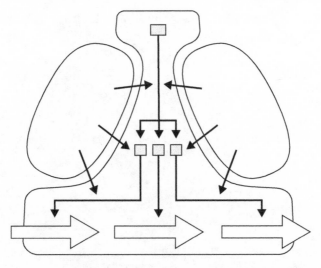

(Logo for the Programmed Machine)

Programmed Machines love hierarchy, order, control, systems, and especially rules, rules, rules. Everything conceivable is programmed, sometimes even the customers. (Have you cleared your tray at a fast-food franchise recently?) All this so that the organization can run as smoothly as a machine. This is why that CEO at GM claimed that uncertainty is the biggest enemy. (Go tell that to an entrepreneur, for whom uncertainty can be the biggest friend. After all, that's how Personal Enterprises beat the Programmed Machines.)

No sport comes close to North American football for its sharp divisions of labor and the extent of its programming. Rules or standards specify who is allowed to hold the ball, catch it, and kick it. Look at the formation on the field, not to mention the cheerleaders on the side: everybody is so carefully lined up. This is not yacht racing, believe me, let alone hockey. Even hierarchy is built right in: the quarterback calls the play, possibly radioed in from the coach, by number no less, and all the players respond accordingly. A sport made to measure for Frederick Taylor's scientific management!

Basic Structure of the Programmed Machine

Every machine has its parts, each specialized to do its bit for the carefully designed whole. (Consider the Administrative Assistant to the Assistant Secretary for Administration.) As Yuval Hariri wrote in his book *Sapiens:* "In bureaucracy, things must be kept apart. There is one drawer for [purchasing, another for manufacturing, a third for selling]. Otherwise, how can you find anything? Things that belong in more than one drawer...are a terrible headache."[51]

In the operating core of the machine organization, jobs are made as simple, specialized, and repetitive as possible, to be done with a minimum of training—often hours, even minutes. (We will come back to football as an exception later.) **Coordination across these jobs is achieved especially by the standardization of work, supported by the standardization of the outputs.** ("Turn that hamburger patty over in 17 seconds.") This enables the bottom managers to supervise a great many workers. Here is a description of a typical Programmed Machine:

> All operations were carried out according to a predetermined plan.... Directions were numerous and explicit, and the work to be done was structured according to task and specialty [with "extensive division of labor"]. The performance of subordinates was closely and efficiently supervised.[52]

This is the temple corporation in ancient Mesopotamia. The Programmed Machine has been around a long time!

If the Personal Enterprise works like a hub, around its chief, then **the Programmed Machine often works like a chain, upon a chain**, as shown in the logo figure. At the base is the *horizontal* chain of work that passes sequentially from one link to the next (as in an automobile assembly line). And laid over this is the *vertical chain of command*, as the managers are stacked up—upon each link and upon each other.

To the left side of the line hierarchy sits the analytical staff who design and control the standards that program the cogs of the machine— people with titles such as work-study analyst, production scheduler, planner, budgeter, and accountant. Hence **the sharpest division of labor in the machine organization is found between the operators who do the work, the managers who administer it, and the analysts who design it.** Nevertheless, **the technostructure emerges as a key part of this organization**. To the line managers may be delegated the formal authority, but to the staff analysts goes the informal power that drives the behavior of everyone else, including the line managers themselves, who also have to adhere to the rules.

> When I was president of this big corporation, we lived in a small Ohio town, where the main plant was located. The corporation specified who you could socialize with, and on what level. (His wife interjects: Who were the wives you could play bridge with.) In a small town they didn't have to keep check on you. Everybody knew. There are certain sets of rules.[53]

In effect, therefore, the machine organization is selectively decentralized, officially to the line managers but substantially to the staff analysts—which gives rise to political games played between line and staff.

On the right side of the figure is the support staff, not powerful so much as abundant, to help maintain the smooth running of the machine—everything from the cafeteria that feeds the people to the legal counsel that handles the lawsuits (of which there can be many). **The proliferation of the support staff is partially explained by the obsession with control in these organizations.** Many of the staff services could be purchased from outside suppliers, but that would expose the organization to the uncertainties of the marketplace. So the inclination has been to *make rather than buy*—in other words, envelope as many of the support services as it can within its own boundaries. (Chapter 20 discusses recent tendencies in the opposite direction.)

Conditions and Kinds of Programmed Machines

Programmed Machines thrive in environments that are simple and stable. The work in complex environments can't be rationalized into simple tasks, while that in dynamic environments can't be predicted, made repetitive, and hence standardized. Thus, don't look for this form of organization in advertising agencies or film companies, but in retailing and fast-moving consumer goods firms (e.g., pens, toothpaste), namely in *mass production* and *mass services*, especially those that pursue a strategy of "cost leadership"—that is, low price.[54]

In addition, this form is frequently found in *mature organizations*, large enough to have the volume of operating work needed for repetition and standardization, and old enough to have settled on the standards they wish to use. These are the organizations that have seen it all before and established procedures to deal with it. Hence, as Personal Enterprises age and grow beyond the control of their founders, many metamorphose into the machine form—at least those that have been functioning in simple environments. And while such a Personal Enterprises may have thrived in a dynamic environment (uncertainty being its best friend), after this kind of transition, the machine form will do what it can to stabilize that environment for the sake of its own programming—for example, develop long-term contracts with suppliers and establish cartels with competitors.

Control enters this picture in other ways, too. **Organizations** *in the* *business of control* **tend to use the machine form**: banks that have to protect people's money, prisons that have to hold inmates, airlines that have to land their passengers safely. As one joke goes, airlines "will soon be moving to a new flight crew, one pilot and a dog. The pilot is there to feed the dog, and the dog is there to bite the pilot if he touches anything."[55]

External control is another condition that drives organizations to the Programmed Machine, because, as discussed in Chapter 6, it acts to centralize and formalize their practices. An owner who wishes to maintain control of a business without managing it appoints a CEO who is held responsible for achieving tight standards of performance. This CEO, in turn, imposes plans and targets down the managerial hierarchy to meet these standards. Taking a company public on the stock market can have the same effect: the market analysts expect a steady growth of earnings. Government departments are likewise driven toward the machine form because politicians and senior civil servants don't like surprises and so encourage the proliferation of rules to avoid them.

But **while some Programmed Machines may be the** *instruments* **of external influencers, others are** *closed systems* **that seek to block out as much outside influence as possible.** Of course, no organization can ever be completely closed. But some machine organizations do come remarkably close—for example, businesses with monopoly positions in their markets. In this regard, don't forget the *Communist regimes* of the twentieth century, which functioned as massive, closed Programmed Machines. (Ironically, the Cold War pitted the

Communist regimes of Eastern Europe against the capitalist corporations of the globalized world, yet structurally, were they that different? As James Worthy, an American executive and writer, commented: "Scientific management had its fullest flowering, not in America, but in Soviet Russia."[56])

Interestingly enough, shifting between being the instrument of an outsider and the closed system of the insiders can be rather easy, because there is no need to change the structure. With formal authority so concentrated at the top of the hierarchy, just bring in a new chief and carry on. (Bring in a new chief in a Personal Enterprise, and everything can be up for grabs.) And don't think this is restricted to business. Many a machine-like NGO, even a whole government taken over by a new political party, has so carried on, perhaps with a new agenda but hardly missing a beat.

Pros and Cons of the Programmed Machine

You don't want your Amazon package delivered to the house next door, or your 8:00 a.m. hotel wake-up call coming at 8:05, any more than you want a guard on your football team to catch a pass from the quarterback. There are rules, after all. **When an integrated set of simple tasks must be performed precisely, predictably, and consistently, at least by animate human beings rather than inanimate machines, the Programmed Machine is unbeatable.**

And, for the same reason, sometimes unbearable too. People can be treated as mechanical parts, but they never are. Nor are they economic things: treating an employee as a *human resource* is like treating a cow as a sirloin steak. I am not a human resource, thank you, nor a human asset or human capital. I am a human being.

Bureaucracy for Better and for Worse

As noted, the word *bureaucracy* is often associated with organizations that function like machines. The term was popularized, innocently enough, by the renowned German sociologist Max Weber, early in the twentieth century, as a neutral, technical term for the kind of organizations we are discussing in this chapter. Weber, in fact, used the word *machine* with regard to its precision and speed: "The fully developed bureaucratic mechanism compares with other organizations exactly as does the machine with the non-mechanical modes of production."[57]

But *bureaucracy* has also taken on a pejorative meaning, as the bad guy of the organizational world, obsessed with control: the executives control the managers, the managers control the workers, the workers control the customers, and the analysts control them all.[58] The planning manager of a British company once remarked that "through the control process, we can stop managers falling in love with their businesses." Should they hate their businesses instead? Michel Crozier concluded in his renowned study of two French government bureaucracies that everyone is treated more or less equally in these organizations because all are controlled by the same overwhelming set of rules.[59] (Like Crozier, it is remarkable how many people rose to prominence in the literature of management by writing about the dysfunctions of machinelike organizations: Mayo, Roethlisberger, Argyris, Bennis, Likert, McGregor, Worthy, and others.)

Today we also use the word *bureaucracy* for government in general, even referring to civil servants as *bureaucrats*—sometimes with the same disparaging undertone. Of course, not all of the public sector is machine bureaucratic (as we shall discuss later), while no few corporations in the private sector are just that. (Read the Dilbert comic strip about bureaucracy in business.)

Let's consider the problems of this form of organization on three levels in the hierarchy.

Alienation in the Operating Core

Frederick Taylor was fond of saying, "In the past the man has been first. In the future, the system must be first." Prophetic words indeed. **For many people, the Programmed Machine is not a happy place to work, especially in its operating core.** To return to James Worthy:

Taylor's view to remove "all possible brain work" from the shop floor also removed all possible initiative from the people who worked there: The "machine has no will of its own. Its parts have no urge to independent action. Thinking, direction—even purpose—must be provided from outside or above." This had the "consequence of destroying the meaning of work itself," which has been "fantastically wasteful for industry and society," resulting in "excessive absenteeism, high worker turnover, sloppy workmanship, costly strikes, even outright sabotage."[60] Wow! And from a corporate executive, no less.

Bear in mind that such criticism has often come from people who are writing, not about their own work, but for the legions of workers made miserable by hyperprogrammed work. For those workers who relish order and predictability, however, the machine organization can be just fine, thank you. Here is how a checker in a supermarket described her work (as quoted in Studs Terkel's wonderful book *Working*):

> They put down their groceries. I got my hips pushin' on the button and it rolls around on the counter. When I feel I have enough groceries in front of me, I let go of my hip. I'm just moving—the hips, the hand, and the register, the hips, the hand, and the register.... (As she demonstrates, her hands and hips move in the manner of an oriental dancer.) You just keep going, one, two, one, two. If you've got that rhythm, you're a fast checker.[61]

Conflict Bumped up the Hierarchy

The operating core of the machine organization is designed to get things done efficiently, not to deal with alienation and conflict. Hence **many human problems that arise in the operations get bumped up the hierarchy, to the managerial middle—straight into the system of silos that hardly encourages the use of mutual adjustment necessary to deal with them.** Too often, the consequence is more conflictive heat than cooperative light.

And so, these conflicts, together with others created by the silos, can get bumped further up the hierarchy, through the *slabs*, until the buck stops at the top, where the silos finally come together. But can a management *above* deal with the problems *below*—ones with which they may lack direct contact?

Disconnect at the "Top"

The answer for the Programmed Machine, once again, is supposed to lie in a system, specifically the *Management Information System* (MIS). It hardens the data generated on the ground, by aggregating it as it mounts the hierarchy, into reports convenient for busy managers to read.

Sales are falling in Indonesia? Tell the manager there to lift them up. But why are they falling? Maybe because the products designed in Iowa are not suited to Indonesian consumers. But the MIS says nothing about that; you have to talk to the customers there to find out. But from a seventy-seventh floor office in New York? Of course, the managers in Indonesia may know why, but where in the MIS are they to enter this information for their bosses at the U.S. HQ?

As Michel Crozier has described the machine organization, "the power of decision . . . tends to be located in a blind spot": "Decisions must be made by people who have no direct knowledge of the field . . . and who must rely on the information given them by subordinates who may have a subjective interest in distorting the data."[62] Or by an MIS that not only aggregates out the necessary details, but also takes time to get its aggregated reports to the management—while more agile competitors may be running off with the customers.

Hard information may help to identify problems, but soft information is necessary to diagnose and resolve them. Lacking that, however, senior managers in the machine organization fall back on the tried if untrue: they tighten the controls, in other words, pour oil on the fire. If, instead, they use direct supervision, they risk being accused of micromanaging: "This is not your Personal Enterprise; respect the hierarchy; focus on the big picture."

To paint a big picture requires mastery of the details, which look awfully hazy from a seventy-seventh floor office. As a result, machine organizations mostly come up with small pictures—marginal adaptations of their existing strategies, or else me-too copies of the strategies of other organizations.

We can call the organizations that do this the *local producers,* of established *industry recipes,* distinguished by *where* they execute them, not *how.*[63] It is certainly efficient to program some standard strategy into your own organization, which is why it is so common. Just have a look at the telephone companies and post offices in different countries, likewise your local grocery store and fitness center.

The machine organization has a way around this. Use Strategic Planning, one of the most popular techniques of all: follow the directions to program the strategy. Unfortunately, Strategic Planning has turned out to be an oxymoron (see box).[64]

STRATEGIC PLANNING IS AN OXYMORON

The central tenet of Strategic Planning is that formulation is separated from implementation. Think, then do. Analyze, then program. Hence it has been especially popular in machine organizations. But such immaculate conception just doesn't hack it in the world of strategy.

When a strategy fails, inevitably the blame is laid on implementation. Could this be because the formulators do the blaming? "You dumbbells weren't smart enough to implement our brilliant strategy." But if these dumbbells were smart, they would retort: "If you're so smart, why didn't you formulate a strategy that we dumbbells were capable of implementing?" You see, every failure of implementation can be described as a failure of formulation.

But what should really be blamed is the very separation of formulation from implementation. This presupposes that the formulator is sufficiently informed, and the situation is sufficiently stable, or predictable, to ensure that no reformulation will be needed during implementation. We have already discussed the problems with both, especially in organizations that are supposed to run like machines. Thus does Strategic Planning become an oxymoron. **Strategies have to be allowed to form, emergently, beyond being formulated, deliberately.**

In contrast, many a remarkable strategy has come from an obscure insight extrapolated into a big picture. IKEA makes unassembled furniture today because a worker tried to put one of its tables into his car and it didn't fit, so he took the legs off. Thus came the strategic moment: "If we have to take the legs off, so do our customers."[65] IKEA was a rather Personal Enterprise at the time, under the control of its founder. Had it been a machine organization, such a message may never have made it through the slabs.

Coming to Terms with Our Machines

We talk incessantly about changing our organizations, especially the machine ones. Is this always necessary? Machines are designed to do specific things. The furnace in our home works very well where it sits, thank you, blowing warm air. I was trained as a mechanical engineer: I suppose I could adapt it to work as a hair dryer. But it's a lot easier to go out and buy one of those instead. By the same token, **why change a Programmed Machine to do what it was not designed to do, instead of concentrating on fine tuning what it does well. Efficiency is its forte, not innovation. An organization cannot put blinders on its people and then expect peripheral vision.**

Generations of planners, consultants, reengineers, and writers have tried to convince us that the Programmed Machine is the default mode of organizing—the all-time one best way. I would guess that 80 percent of everything ever written about fixing organizations has been written about machine organizations, although not recognized as such, whether to tighten those controls and plan everything in sight, or else cope with the consequences of these controls and plans by bringing in that maintenance crew for the human machinery.

I'm not one for "five easy steps" to do anything in organizations, but I make an exception with this box for any chief determined to fix his or her organization, quickly.

FIVE EASY STEPS TO FIX YOUR ORGANIZATION (any one will do)

1. Treat human beings as human resources. Fire them in great numbers when the organization has not met its numbers, even if that's your fault.
2. Ignore the organization's past, its history and culture. Bring in a whole new "top team" who, not knowing the place, will measure like mad.
3. Move all the managers around so that they can never get to know anything but management well. And if you are the CEO of a corporation, kick yourself upstairs, where you can be the leader of a portfolio instead of the manager of a real business. (If you are heading up another kind of organization, call yourself CEO to pretend that you are running a business.)
4. As the problems from doing all this mount up, go for the quick fix: hire consultants to program anything still unprogrammed.
5. Finally, be sure to do everything in five easy steps.

All four forms of organizations have their pros as well as their cons. The machine organization may not be the one best way to organize, but it is one important way. **So long as we demand inexpensive, mass-produced products and services, which can be provided more efficiently by people than by actual machines, the Programmed Machine will remain with us—with all its faults.**

As you may have gathered, this is not where I prefer to work. (That's coming next.) But I do appreciate these machines for flying to conferences and printing books. I cannot live without them even though I choose not to work within them. And like most everyone, I had better not kid myself into thinking that other people are the bureaucrats. **We are all the bureaucrats—you and I—when insisting on adherence to the rules for the sake of some order we wish to preserve.**

CHAPTER 9

The Professional Assembly

The most powerful drive in the ascent of people is the pleasure in their own skill. They love to do what they do well, and having done it, they love to do it better.
—Jacob Bronowski

My dictionary defines an *assembly* as "a body of persons gathered together for a purpose." This is rather close to the definition of *organization* given in Chapter 1—as collective action structured for the pursuit of common mission. But in some organizations, the people gather together less closely than in others. Welcome to the Professional Assembly.

Here, skilled people assemble to carry out their services: educate students, transplant hearts, make music, play baseball. It may look

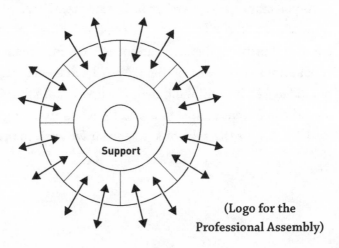

(Logo for the
Professional Assembly)

like they are working together, but mostly they are working apart, co-ordinated almost automatically by the standardization of their skills, based on their extensive training.

Watch an orchestra in concert, or an ant colony in action, and you will see amazing coordination without the need to exchange a single comment or take a single order. Is the double play in baseball any different? The shortstop picks up the ball and flips it to the second baseman, who throws out the player at first base. The beauty is in the execution, not the innovation, just as in open-heart surgery. (Would you like to be operated on by a creative surgeon? Does your favorite baseball team have a creative shortstop?)

Can you imagine any other team sport more individualistic than baseball? The players all stand apart, each to do his or her own thing. (Compare this with a scrum in rugby.) No one on the field is in charge, even the manager in the dugout dresses like the players. At bat the players come up one by one and run the bases alone. Everyone is in a personal silo. This has to be the best sport to play during a pandemic, leaving aside virtual chess.

Basic Structure of the Professional Assembly
Coordination through Training to Standardize the Skills

How do a hundred musicians on a stage, even a handful of health-care professionals in an operating room, coordinate so precisely? Not by mutual adjustment, certainly not by direct supervision, the conductor notwithstanding. The answer lies in **training, the key design parameter of the Professional Assembly. Here is where the skills and knowledge of the operating workers are standardized,** whether as scores in music, protocols in medicine, or principles of accounting. A cardiovascular surgeon described the "cookbook" he developed for his work, in which he listed, even for "complex operations," the essential steps as chains of thirty to forty symbols on a single sheet, to "be reviewed mentally in sixty to 120 seconds at some time during the day preceding the operation."[66] Talk about standardization!

While the work standards used in the Programmed Machine are developed by analysts in its own technostructure, **the skill standards used in the Professional Assembly are imported from the outside, through the hiring of people educated in a university or specialized institution, followed by substantial training on the job,** such as an internship in medicine, where the knowledge is applied and the skills are practiced. The professionals spend all these years learning not only what they have to do, but also what their colleagues will be doing, so that they can achieve that almost automatic coordination. This was captured perfectly in a *New Yorker* cartoon that showed several physicians surrounding a patient on an operating table, with the line "Who opens?" The Professional Assembly is not a game of bridge: they all know perfectly well who opens.

All this has the effect of freeing the professionals from significant control by analysts in their own organization. But not from external control by their own professional associations, which establish, enforce, and update these standards. Hence, expect open-heart surgery in one hospital to look much like that in another, likewise Ravel's *Boléro* played by one orchestra to another. What better illustration of this than a guest conductor, who arrives days earlier to conduct a concert. Can you imagine a "guest manager" in any other form of organization?

So **while the machine organization defers to the authority of office, the professional organization defers to the autonomy of expertise. These are *meritocracies*.** Yet they, too, tend to have large operating units, thanks to the standardization. Hence a hundred musicians can work with one conductor, a likewise number of my colleagues with one dean.

The Autonomy of the Professionals

The hospital was used in Chapter 2 as an example of a hub, with the staff coming to and going from the building as well as the patient. But that is physical movement. **In its functioning, the Professional**

Assembly is structured as a set of relatively autonomous professionals. When I did conventional teaching, I cannot recall a colleague or dean ever visiting my classroom. I closed the door and did my thing.

I like to say that the reason I chose to work in a professional organization is that it is the only place where I can be self-employed yet draw a regular salary. Well, not quite self-employed, but still rather independent. Our faculty does not work like a trucking company, although one business school I know appointed the ex-CEO of a trucking company as dean. He claimed that managing professors was just like managing truckers—hence many of the best trucker-professors left. (Earlier in his life, he might have been that student described in Chapter 1 who studied a symphony orchestra.)

Speaking of a symphony orchestra, watch one in performance, this marvel of coordination. The musicians hardly look at the conductor, let alone at each other. The great maestro on the podium seen as the epitome of leadership is pure myth.[67] Tchaikovsky is pulling the strings, not Toscanini. (As he, himself, said: "I am no genius. I have created nothing. I play the music of other men."[68]) Each musician is playing the notes written for his or her instrument by the composer. But the composer is dead, so the audience, enthralled by the music, heaps its praise on the conductor. (Later we shall consider the conductor's role *off* the podium—it's more managerial than magisterial.)

Highly Decentralized

The Professional Assembly is the most decentralized of all four forms of organization, for the professionals at least. Not only do they have this autonomy, but together they exercise considerable power over many of the administrative decisions that affect them—often the hiring of new colleagues, even the selection of their own managers. That results, for them at least, in a highly democratic, decentralized structure. A hundred of us at McGill can report to one dean because in practice we hardly need to report to her at all. In many hospitals, the physicians don't even report officially into the administrative hierarchy, although they are acutely aware of their own hierarchy of professional status—upward, from interns to residents to staff physicians to the research stars.

Hence these organizations are sometimes described as upside-down pyramids, with the professionals on top and the administrators below, to serve them—for example, by raising money. But not so fast. As shown in the logo diagram on the first page of this chapter, the hierarchy is not upside-down so much as flat. And for the less skilled staff, who are more conventionally supervised, and are often jerked around by the professionals as well, this democracy can feel more like oligarchy.

Substantial Support Staff

Because the standards are largely established and enforced externally, the professional organization has relatively little need for the analytical staff of a technostructure. There is always some—every organization needs budgeting people to control spending, for example—but their influence tends to be limited by the power of the operating professionals.

The support staff in the Professional Assembly is, however, another story. **Given the high cost of professionals, it makes sense to back them up with as much support as possible**. Thus universities have libraries, alma mater funds, faculty clubs, publishing houses, archives, and many other support units, their people numbering far more than the professors.

Tailored Customization

Consider how the four forms of organization diagnose client requests for their services. There is little diagnosis in the machine organization: it is programmed to respond to each stimulus, much as we do when tapped on the knee (tap McDonald's for a Big Mac and out it comes; "Sorry, we don't do tapenade"). In contrast, as we shall see, the project organization engages in fully open-ended diagnosis: given a request, it goes for a customized solution. And in the personal organization, diagnosis is whatever the chief chooses it to be, standardized or customized.

In the professional organization we find something between pure standardization and pure customization—what we earlier called *tailored customization*. The standards are adjusted to the need at hand, as when a stent is chosen to fit a particular artery, or an outfielder in baseball decides whether to throw the ball to third base or home plate, depending on the speed of the runner. Accordingly, no matter how standardized the skills, the complexity of the work mandates a certain degree of discretion in their application. No two professionals—surgeons, professors, social workers—apply them in exactly the same way: many judgments are required, sometimes improvisations as well.

This tailored standardization gives rise to what especially distinguishes this form of organization. **The Professional Assembly functions by *pigeonholing*—that is, by putting the need of the user into the category of the professional.** Present yourself to a hospital with a pain in your lower right side, and in minutes you may find yourself on an operating table with your appendix being removed (according to the protocol of some professional association). Register for a bachelor's degree in philosophy, physics, or physiotherapy, and out comes the syllabus of standard courses from which to choose.

To sum up its structure, **the logo on the first page of this chapter shows the Professional Assembly as a set of autonomous professionals, assigned to their specialized units but facing out to whomever they serve, with not much of an administrative hierarchy or technostructure, but a substantial support staff.**

Conditions and Kinds of Professional Assemblies

Organizations whose operating work is complex enough to require extensive training yet stable enough to be able to do it with limited customization are drawn to the Professional Assembly. Hence our examples have included hospitals, universities, accounting firms, orchestras, and baseball teams—all but the last two, *personal service organizations*. But the professional organization can be found in manufacturing too, where the above conditions hold, as in *craft enterprises* that use skilled workers to produce, say, handmade glassware. **The very term *craft* implies a kind of professional who learns traditional skills through long apprentice training.** Craft enterprises tend to have relatively few administrators, who, in fact, may work alongside the operating craftspeople.

Because of the reliance on professional skills, the technology used in the operating core of the Professional Assembly can be rather simple, as in education and baseball. Traditional forms of surgery often relied on the scalpel, although these days most surgery depends on a lot of fancy equipment.

Pros and Cons of the Professional Assembly

This form of organization is unique among the four in responding to two paramount interests of many people working in organizations today: democracy and autonomy. By having the best of these two worlds, the professionals can be highly motivated, and deeply dedicated to their work. Unlike the Programmed Machine, which places barriers between the worker and whoever is served, this form removes them. But in these characteristics of democracy and autonomy lie three paramount problems of the Professional Assembly: categorization, discretion, and change. As you read this, you may wish to keep in mind various quotes about experts (see box).

SOME QUOTES ABOUT EXPERTS

"An expert is someone with no elementary knowledge."

"An expert avoids all of the many pitfalls on his or her way to the grand fallacy."

"For every expert, there is an equal and opposite expert."
(Arthur C. Clarke)

"The meaning of [the PhD] is that the recipient of instruction is examined for the last time in [their] life, and is pronounced completely full. After this, no new ideas can be imparted to [them]." (Stephen Leacock)

"Training is everything. The peach was once a bitter almond; cauliflower is nothing but cabbage with a college education." (Mark Twain)

"Experts are people who know more and more about less and less until finally they know everything about nothing. Well, then, if managers are people who know less and less about more and more until finally they know nothing about everything, what happens when the experts and the managers meet?"

The Problems of Categorization

The standardization of skills is a loose coordinating mechanism at best, inadequate to cope with ambiguities that arise at the margins, between the pigeonholes. Much political blood is thus spilled over categories that are either imperfectly conceived or artificially distinguished. I recall a dispute in a hospital about who should be doing the mastectomies: gynecologists who treat women or surgeons who do operations. In a management school that has no course in organization studies, where should this book be used: in organization behavior or strategic management? And when a baseball is hit exactly between the center and right fielder, who should catch it? This is one of the few times when they may talk to each other—that is, use mutual adjustment—or else make the evening news when the ball falls between them.

   In medicine especially, with its increasing hyperspecialization, **categorization is its great strength as well as its debilitating weakness.**[69] When the categories fit, medicine is brilliant. With an appendix about to burst, out it comes. Unfortunate, however, are those patients whose needs fall *beyond the categories*, *across the categories*, and *beneath the categories*.

   Beyond the categories are those illnesses for which there is no

disease—meaning that medicine has no category to treat what the patient experiences. For example, irritable bowel syndrome—a label for
our ignorance—is felt acutely by many untreated people. Across the
categories fall those patients, often geriatric, who have to be treated
for multiple diseases concurrently. This requires coordination by mutual adjustment, which many physicians resist. Finally are those *patients* who need to be treated as *people*: their diseases require personal
consideration beneath the established medical categories, or, if you
like, past what the protocols prescribe.[70]

The Problem of Discretion

"Power tends to corrupt, and absolute power corrupts absolutely."
So said Lord Acton. Few players in organizations have more discre-
tionary power than the professionals in their assemblies. Discretion
works well when they are competent and conscientious. But how to
deal, for example, with those physicians who mistreat their clients
(in both senses of the word)? The administrators have relatively little
control over them, while their colleagues, even their professional associations, can be reluctant to censure them. In universities, the term
ivory tower is indicative of the tendency to look down rather than to
reach out. Professors, for example, expect to be the sole judges of
their own scholarship when they publish exclusively in their "peer-
reviewed" journals.[71]

    **Compounding this problem of discretion is the difficulty of mea-
suring the performance of professionals**. Can we really measure how
much a child actually learns in a classroom, beyond what is parroted
back on an exam? Early in the days of liver transplants, a surgeon operated on ten patients. Eight survived, but one needed a new transplant,
and another had a recurrence of an earlier cancer, while all but three of
the rest were too sick to resume work. When asked about his performance, the surgeon claimed 8/10, and, if he did that second transplant,
9/11. (He counted livers, not people!) An administrator said 6/10, while
for the nurses, it was 3/10.[72] And the correct answer is...

Do you need a really good surgeon for a difficult operation? Let me suggest that you find one with a high death rate. Not because you want an inferior surgeon, but because you need one who has taken on the most difficult cases. There are reports of surgeons who have avoided such cases to keep that number low.

Most commonly, discretion allows professionals to ignore the needs of the organization itself. Loyalty is usually stronger to the profession than the place where it is practiced. But Professional Assemblies need loyalty too—for example, to staff their administrative committees, especially in times of significant change.

The Problem of Administrative Change

The categories tend to be rather firm in the Professional Assembly. But significant change requires a rearrangement of the categories, and that requires the collaboration of the professionals who have so much of the power in these organizations, yet are used to working individually, and stably. True, their work may be changing all the time— new protocols in medicine, new theories in universities—but this is change at the margins, usually *within* the categories (called *paradigms* in the world of academia). Hence **Professional Assemblies are highly resistant to administrative change**, perhaps even more so than the Programmed Machines, which at least concentrate the power for change atop their hierarchies of authority.

Mistreating the Professional Assembly Itself

Because some professionals mistreat the people they are supposed to serve, outside influencers who pay the bills (governments, donors, insurance companies, egged on by management consultants and board members from business) often retort by mistreating the professional organization. They foist technocratic controls on it—for example, performance measures galore—driving it to function like a Programmed Machine, which often exacerbates the very problems they are trying to fix. (Did you ever meet a number that cannot be gamed, especially by a clever professional?) Or they try to have it fixed with the latest management technique, designed to make factories efficient, or machines strategic. All of this is predicated on the assumption of power at the top, hence the reliance on a determined chief to bring some order to the place. **Perhaps nothing has broken the spirit of our professional services—in schools especially—more than these imposed technocratic fixes.**[73]

This "business is best" way of thinking has driven many professionals, especially teachers and professors, to unionize, which has done further damage to their institutions, by driving in deeper the wedge between them and the administrators. These institutions function on the basis of individual responsibility more than collective action. But having to present a united front in its collective bargaining, the unions focus on concerns that are collective, such as remuneration. The direct effect can be to drive whatever remains of the Professional Assembly further toward the Programmed Machine, which may be the inverse of why the professionals unionized in the first place.[74]

By recognizing the pros and cons of each form of organization, we can avoid trying to fix one in the mind-set of another. It is not governments that educate the children, not insurance companies that deliver the babies, not donors who play the symphonic music. These things are done by professionals, in their assemblies. **If a professional is irresponsible or incompetent, no measure, no plan, no rule fashioned in some technostructure, no order from someone in authority, can ever make that person responsible, let alone competent. But such measures, plans, rules, and orders can distract the responsible professionals from performing effectively.**

To paraphrase that old nursery rhyme, when the professionals are good, they are very, very good. But when they're bad, they're horrid. **When the external influencers misunderstand the professional organization, they can make even the good professionals horrid.**

CHAPTER 10

The Project Pioneer

"It's all so simple, Anjiin-san, just change your concept of the world . . ."

—So said the Japanese lady to her confused British lover,
shipwrecked in the novel *Shogun*

In his introduction to *Winnie-the-Pooh*, A. A. Milne wrote that "There are some people who begin the Zoo at the beginning, called WAYIN, and walk as quickly as they can past every cage until they get to the one called WAYOUT, but the nicest people go straight to the animal they love the most, and stay there."[75] Without claiming to be a nice person, I must admit that this is the organizational beast I love the most—at least to write about, if not to work in. I don't need that much excitement, thank you.[76]

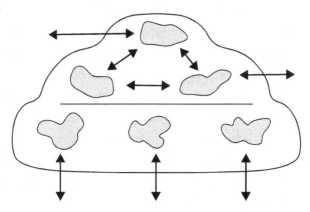

(Logo for the Project Pioneer)

None of the organization forms discussed so far is capable of so-phisticated innovation, the kind required of a high-tech research lab, an avant garde film company, a factory that makes complex proto-types, even a hockey team determined to beat a stronger opponent. The Personal Enterprise can certainly innovate—if the chief is so inclined—but usually in simpler ways, while the Programmed Ma-chine and Professional Assembly are performance organizations, not problem-solving ones. They are designed to exploit standardized products and procedures, more than invent new ones. **The Project Pioneers are the explorers of the modern world, staffed with *intra-preneurial experts* who collaborate to create novel outputs**—ones that open new territory.

Let's come back to diagnosis, as introduced earlier. There is none to speak of in the Programmed Machine, which tends to respond to expected stimuli automatically. It is limited in the Professional As-sembly, which prefers to pigeonhole user needs into established cat-egories. We can sometimes see more open diagnosis in the Personal Enterprise, for simpler problems. But it is in the Project Pioneer that we find diagnosis in its full flowering, as open-ended problem solving, to encourage the development of fully customized solutions.

Sports as Projects

In football, the quarterback (or coach) calls the pre-programmed play and the players respond accordingly. In baseball, the way the ball is hit usually determines how the play unfolds. **In hockey, basketball, rugby, and soccer, however, when a team picks up the puck or ball at its end, nobody quite knows how the play will unfold—the players included, who have to collaborate spontaneously to outwit their opponent. It's like a new project every time.**

The essence of these sports is to take advantage of the situation at hand, including the strengths and weaknesses of the players on both sides as well as the opportunities that open up. Of course, there can be surprises in the other sports too, but they tend to be the exceptions more than the rule. **In a project organization, expect the unexpected.** No scorecard to fill in here, as in baseball—what would the categories be anyway? And in hockey, who could write that fast? (Soccer is like hockey in slow motion, while baseball has been described as watching the grass grow.)

Robert Keidel has written that "basketball is too dynamic a sport to permit the rigid separation of planning and execution that characterizes football.... Quoting one famous player: 'Your game plan may be wiped out by what happens in the first minute of play.' Success... depends on the ability of the coach and players to plan and adjust while in motion."[77] Of course, there are times when one player does it all. But mostly, these are intensely collaborative team sports: indeed, there can be as much beauty in the passing as in the scoring.

Adhocracy

The Project Pioneer is depicted in the logo for this chapter as a web—namely, a network of open-ended mutual adjustments. If, at the limit, the Personal Enterprise can be described as *autocracy*, the Programmed Machine as *bureaucracy*, and the Professional Assembly as *meritocracy*, then the Project Pioneer is *adhocracy*.[78]

Years ago, I submitted an article for publication that used the word *adhocracy*.[79] From the editor came this question: "What's adhocracy?" I didn't quite understand: I thought the description was clear enough. Anyway, I fixed it up a bit and resubmitted the article. Back came this reply: "We're ready to go, just one last question: What's adhocracy?" "Wait a minute," I pleaded, "we've been through this already." The editor looked over the comments she had received from her colleagues, and when she came to "Is this the lack of structure?" I suddenly understood. The problem lay not with adhocracy but with bureaucracy. To many management consultants, government officials, and corporate CEOs, let alone magazine editors, the Programmed Machine *is* organization. Adhocracy must therefore be *disorganization*.

Not at all. **Top-down control, unity of command, strategic plan-**

ning, formalization of procedure: the Project Pioneer violates all these tenets of the Programmed Machine. But if we turn all this on its head, we get, not the lack of structure, but another structure, no less viable in its own context: the Project Pioneer.[80]

Basic Structure of the Project Pioneer

The Project Pioneer, like the Personal Enterprise, has a loose, organic structure, but whereas the latter coordinates largely by the direct supervision of a chief, **the Project Pioneer relies for coordination on mutual adjustment within and across its teams of experts.** It does so to achieve difficult innovation. Years ago, when I approached a company that used this structure, asking for a copy of its organization chart, I received this reply: "We would prefer not to supply an organization chart, since it would change too quickly to serve any useful purpose." I never asked that question of an adhocracy again!

Here we find little technostructure, not much beyond using budgets and schedules to try to keep the projects on track—no easy matter. On several occasions I have been invited to do workshops in such organizations, to legitimize the notion of adhocracy. My favorite question has always been: "Who's the most miserable person in an adhocracy?" This was inevitably followed by a brief silence, then growing laughter as everyone looked at some poor soul cowering in a corner: the controller, of course. Someone has to keep the lid on all the volatility.

Support staff do, however, figure prominently in the project organization, but not as in the machine and professional organizations. Here is where many of the experts are housed, in specialized units, to be deployed on the project teams to add their knowledge—for example, a scientist in research to a team developing a new product. Hence, the support staff are not off to one side, to speak only when spoken to; they are part and parcel of the project structure. With everyone pitching in on those teams, how is line to be distinguished from staff anyway?

Not only is the distinction between line and staff blurred in the Project Pioneer, but so are all the formal distinctions of conventional organizations. This enables the experts to move freely about the place, as do basketball players on the court. Accordingly, the project organization is selectively decentralized: power flows to whoever can deal with whatever is necessary at the moment, managers and nonmanagers alike.

The connecting of the support staff is an indication of the extensive use of matrix structure in the Project Pioneers. Hence, managers abound in these organizations: functional managers, integrating managers, and especially project managers, because the project teams have to be kept small to facilitate coordination by mutual adjustment.

But the managers of the Project Pioneer tend not to manage in the conventional sense. They connect more than control, especially across the teams. In other words, they coordinate by mutual adjustment more than dictate by direct supervision. Indeed, they, too, often work as regular members of the project teams. Some years ago, when I was observing the chief operating officer of a large high-tech software company in France, he joined the meeting of a project team. When I asked why, he explained that the team was developing some new software that would set a precedent for the company—in his words, it was "the beginning of a strategy"—and therefore needed his active participation.[81] As we shall discuss in Chapter 11, strategies emerge in project organizations through this kind of grounded learning.

To summarize, the Project Pioneer functions as an organic mass of operating experts, line managers, and staff specialists who work together in ever-shifting relationships on ad hoc project teams.

Conditions and Kinds of Project Pioneers

Project Pioneers tend to be found in environments that are both complex and dynamic, from high technology to guerrilla warfare. The

complexity requires experts, and the dynamism requires team-work among them.

Notice that most of the examples used in this chapter thus far are in industries that have developed since the latter part of the twentieth century, many of them in high technology. **We live in an era of adhocracy, at least for much of what is new in our world of organizations.** Hence the literature has come up with many labels for this form (see box).

ADHOCRACY BY ANY OTHER NAME?

- Network Organization
- Temporary Organization
- Ambidextrous Organization
- Lattice Organization
- Spiderweb Organization
- Task Force Organization
- Cluster Organization[82]

There are *permanent adhocracies* that reorganize from one project to the next, and *temporary adhocracies* that engage in one major project and then disband—such as an Olympic Organizing Committee. **There are also *operating adhocracies* that undertake projects for outsiders, and *administrative adhocracies* whose projects serve themselves.** Thus, a jazz quartet is an operating adhocracy: it plays creatively for its audience, just as a design studio develops new products for its clients. Companies in gaming, on the other hand, undertake a steady stream of projects to bring new products to the marketplace, even if they manufacture them in machine-like structures, or outsource this manufacturing altogether. In other words, administrative adhocracies sell the products, not the projects. Aircraft manufacturers do likewise, although when they customize a corporate jet for a particular buyer, they are functioning as an operating adhocracy. The logo for this chapter shows these two forms of Project Pioneers, one with the projects in the operating core, the other with them distributed across their administration.

Adhocracy also appears, in the administrative form, when a machine organization that automates its operations shifts toward the project form. As described in Chapter 6, with machinery replacing the people who were doing routine operating work, the focus of the organization shifts to skilled specialists who collaborate in teams to design, develop, and maintain that machinery.

Mention should also be made here of *extended adhocracies*, which further blur the boundaries of this form. Being so flexible, Project Pioneers are inclined to welcome outsiders on their project teams, for example to use their specialized expertise. Not infrequently, they also outsource some aspects of their projects entirely, as do aircraft manufacturers with the design and fabrication of the engines for their new planes. (We shall return to this outsourcing in Chapter 20.)

The Cons of the Project Pioneer

We have discussed the pros of the Project Pioneer at some length; the cons are perhaps less appreciated than those of the other three forms, thanks to it being in fashion. Even for this reason alone, these cons deserve more careful consideration.

The Project Pioneer is no utopia. It has its strengths, in its place, like the other forms, and its faults beyond these. In particular, **the ambiguities of the project organization can be unnerving, and too much efficiency can be sacrificed for the sake of effectiveness.**

Ubiquitous Ambiguity

It has been said that if you can't stand the heat, get out of the kitchen. **If you can't stand the ambiguities, get out of the project organization.** We all appreciate novelty, but so too do we crave stability. An unrelenting pace of change can get to people after a while, as can the opposite. In January everyone is working frantically to finish a project; by March they are playing cards for want of work. Boom and bust. Can we blame those who crave the steadier life of a Professional Assembly, or a CEO who grabs an opportunity to mass produce a particularly successful product and be done with all the innovating?

Even within ongoing projects, there can be considerable anxiety. Will it work? What if the necessary creativity doesn't materialize? Who belongs where in the abstruse matrix structure? All this can be a breeding ground for conflict. But **with power so diffused amid the ambiguities of the project organization, political games arise naturally and focus can get lost.**

Inefficient Effectiveness

Project Pioneers are not much good at doing ordinary things; they relish the extraordinary. But novelty is messy and can be time-consuming. Squeezing the teams to be efficient, or taking away their slack, can kill their creativity. **The Project Pioneer gains its effectiveness by being *inefficient*.** With a variety of people having to function in ad hoc teams—operators, line managers, and staff experts, inside and outside the organization—much time has to be spent on communication. That's not efficient. Moreover, to be innovative, people have to learn together from their mistakes, and this means being able—even encouraged—to make mistakes and have the time to correct them.

A meeting of the team is called about some unanticipated problem. It gets defined and redefined. Eventually solutions are generated, debated, and discarded or embraced. All this while alliances are building amid hard bargaining. Finally, a decision emerges—that in itself is an accomplishment—although it is likely to be late and modified later, eventually to prove pioneering.

Expect to see a lot more of adhocracy!

CHAPTER 11

The Four Together

How basic are these four forms? Basic indeed. One is personal. One is programmed. One is professional. One is project. Are they real? That, as we shall see, depends on what we mean by *real*.

Four Forms Forever

These forms can be seen to go way back, to when humans first became organized. The project organization, of "our age," is probably the oldest, when Homo sapiens hunted collaboratively in packs (i.e., teams). As people settled into communities, leadership in the form of the personal organization arose. We have already seen an example of the programmed organization in ancient Mesopotamia, where there was also suggestion of the professional one: "Skilled artisans were frequently recruited from distant regions. Workers were organized into guilds by specialty."[83]

As for the heyday of the forms, if today is the era of the project organization, then perhaps that of the personal organization was when monarchs and feudal lords ruled. The Industrial Revolution brought in that of the programmed organization, which likely persists as highly prominent, even if the Personal Enterprise may be the most ubiquitous.[84] (Think of all the sovereigns, autocrats, entrepreneurs, and tycoons. "Master" is a heading in my thesaurus for twenty-one categories of this, which cover a page-and-a-half! We remain obsessed with leadership.) There may not have been a heyday for the professional organization, but it did spread as the professions established themselves in the twentieth century.

Heydays of structural fashion notwithstanding, all four forms are prominent today, and will remain so, as suggested by the many current examples in the last four chapters. How do you identify a form that might fit when you encounter an organization (see box)?

WHAT FORM IS IT?

Ask a few questions about an organization to see if one of the four forms might fit, more or less.

- Is most of the key work in the operating core simple and repetitive (e.g., mass production or the mass distribution of services)? If so, look for a Programmed Machine.
- Otherwise, is the most important work in the operating core rather skilled, yet stable? If so, look for a Professional Assembly.
- And if the most important work, whether in the operating core or the administration, is carried out in collaborative teams for customized results, look for a Project Pioneer.
- Apart from all this, or in spite of it, if one person holds the lion's share of the power in the organization, look for a Personal Enterprise.

Alternately, *see* the form. Close your eyes and imagine what living thing best describes your organization—an ant colony or an elephant, a mushroom or a tree, whatever. Can you see one of the forms in your metaphor?

Summarizing the Forms

We know a good deal about these four forms: the structures they use, their processes to form strategies, the nature of their managers' work, the problems they tend to encounter, and so on. Table 11.1 summarizes this. For the most part, the table can speak for itself (extrapolated

Table 11.1 The Four Forms of Organization

FORM	Personal Enterprise	Programmed Machine	Professional Assembly	Project Pioneer
At the extreme	Autocracy	Bureaucracy	Meritocracy	Adhocracy
Shape	Chief at the center of a hub	Chain of command atop chain of operations	Set of autonomous professionals	Web of teams
Favored coordinating mechanism	Direct supervision	Standardization of work	Standardization of skills	Mutual adjustment
Structure	Simple, flexible, centralized, can be one large group	Formalized, hierarchical, limited decentralization (to analysts)	Decentralized to the professionals, who work in large functional units	Liaison devices, matrix structure, decentralized to small teams
Standardization / Customization	Some customization	Standardization	Tailored customization	Customization
Conditions	Simple, dynamic environment, often small in size	Simple, stable environment, mature, external control	Complex, stable environment	Complex, dynamic (high technology) environment, automation, fashionable
Variants	Entrepreneurial firm Start-up Turnaround Small organization	Mass production Mass service Instrument Closed system Local producer Snappy bureaucracy	Professional service Craft producer	Operating adhocracy Administrative adhocracy Extended adhocracy Mammoth project Platform organization
Main force	Consolidation	Efficiency	Proficiency	Collaboration
Buzzwords	Charisma, vision, turnaround	Silos, TQM, restructuring, empowerment, benchmarking, time studies, strategic planning, reengineering, value chain, downsizing, fine tuning	Knowledge work, teleworking, credentials, pigeonholing, collegiality	Teamwork, networking, matrix structure, project management, intrapreneurship, championing, partnerships, learning organization

(continued)

Table 11.1 *(continued)*

FORM	Personal Enterprise	Programmed Machine	Professional Assembly	Project Pioneer
Decision making	Seeing first (art)	Thinking first (science/analysis)	Thinking first (craft/science, evidence-based)	Doing first (craft, experience-based)
Strategy making	Visioning (deliberate perspective, emergent positions)	Planning (deliberate positions)	Venturing (emergent positions)	Learning (emergent positions and perspective)
Strategies	Niche, narrow scope	Cost leadership	Multiple positions	Differentiation, exploration
Pros	Responsive, dedicated, directed	Efficient, reliable, precise	Dedicated, proficient	Innovative, flexible, engaging
Cons	Restricted, precarious	Impersonal, inflexible	Disjointed, conflictive	Inefficient, ambiguous, tendency to drift
Managing	Irrepressible	Exceptional	External	Engaged
Key managerial roles	Doing, dealing, and controlling inside	Controlling	Communicating, linking, and dealing	Doing, linking, dealing, and communicating

from comments in the last four chapters), save for a few explanatory words below, except for two of the characteristics that will be discussed at greater length: the strategy processes and managerial work in each of the forms.

Figure 11.1 plots the four forms of organization on the triangle of art-craft-science, with the Personal Enterprise shown closest to art (the vision of the chief) and the Programmed Machine closest to science (in its use of analysis), while the Professional Assembly functions between science and craft (evidence and experience), and the Project Pioneer is perhaps closer to craft (experience-based teamwork), but with the creative use of art as well.

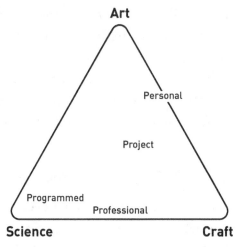

FIGURE 11.1 The Forms on the Triangle

Buzzwords (tools, techniques, concepts) are listed under the form where they seem to be most commonly found—for example, charismatic leadership in the personal organization and knowledge work in the professional one. That so many are listed under the Programmed Machine is another indication of the extent to which this form dominates our thinking about organizations.

Strategy Formation in the Forms

Chapter 3 introduced four approaches to the development of strategy, labeled planning (deliberate, about positions), visioning (deliberate, about perspective, with positions emerging), venturing (emergent, about positions), and learning (emergent, about positions and perspective). These map remarkably well onto the four forms of organizations—in fact, they may be the most revealing of the differences between them.

Visioning Strategy by the Chief of the Personal Enterprise

In the Personal Enterprise, strategy tends to take the form of the vision of the chief, as in the case of a Steve Jobs at Apple. Such a vision can be highly deliberate, and tightly integrated. As a strategic perspective, it serves as an umbrella under which specific strategic positions can emerge (at Apple: laptops, iPads, watches, etc.). In the Personal Enterprise, these strategies are often found in niches that enable the organization to escape the competition of the established machines—for example, a restaurant that focuses on organic offerings.

Planning Positions in the Programmed Machine

As noted, machine organizations have long been the champions of Strategic Planning, whereby senior managers are expected to formulate deliberate strategies for everyone else to implement. But as indicated in Chapter 8, **all too often strategic planning reduces to strategic programming, namely extrapolating the consequences of a strategic perspective already in place** (positions to add, expenses to cut, and so on). Put differently, numbers tend to dominate, often with barely a new idea, let alone a renewed vision, in sight. Here, then, the strategic plans, so called, reduce to *action* plans, backed up by performance controls.[85]

Where, then, does the strategic perspective come from? Frequently from an earlier time, as a Personal Enterprise, when the founding chief developed it. Or else, not uncommonly, it has been copied from other organizations in the industry, as a me-too strategy.

Of course, a machine can always be fine-tuned: there is always room for new strategic positions (adding Egg McMuffin to the McDonald's menu). But don't look for strategic revolutions here, at least so long as the organization maintains its machine characteristics. **Change an element of a tightly integrated machine and it can disintegrate.**

Venturing Positions at the Base of the Professional Assembly

Even more me-too are the overall strategies of the Professional Assemblies. Because so much of what they do is regulated by their common professional associations, these organizations tend to be the local providers of generic strategies. Just compare your local general hospital with others across town, or your local university with others around the world: it may well be distinguished by *where* it provides its services more than by *what* services it provides.

Janet Rose and I tracked the strategic activities of McGill University across a century and a half of its history.[86] In all that time the university managed to close only one faculty—Veterinary Medicine, which lasted barely a decade and a half. The university proved to be the sum total of every faculty it ever had!

Yet **lurking beneath the surface of many a standard-looking professional organization can be all sorts of unique strategic positions, championed by the operating professionals.** Seen from a distance, McGill has all the usual faculties—Arts, Science, Medicine, Management, and so on. But look more closely within them, and you will find many unique programs, such as our International Master's Program for Managers (impm.org), which has none of the usual courses in marketing and finance, nor young students sitting in U-shaped classrooms discussing cases. Instead, midcareer managers sit at roundtables where they learn from their own experience, in modules labeled reflection, analysis, collaboration, worldliness, and change.

Such ventures abound in Professional Assembles, but few come from their management: most are championed by the operating professionals within their own specialties. Can the sum of all such ventures really be said to add up to a strategy for these organizations? Yes indeed, because together they determine how it positions itself in its environment.[87] **Just as it assembles its people into its structure, so too does the Professional Assembly assemble its strategic positions into its overall strategy.**

Learning Strategies across the Project Pioneer

Strategy is learned in the Project Pioneer as its teams build on their experience. Of course, strategies are learned in the Personal

Enterprise as well—it, too, can explore—but through the personal experience of an individual chief. Hence its strategy is likely to be more integrated than that learned from the various team efforts of the project organization.

We studied the strategic history of the National Film Board of Canada, an agency of the federal government of Canada that had become renowned for its short documentary films.[88] Here was the quintessential adhocracy, each film a project in its own right. At one point, the NFB suddenly branched into feature films, a brand-new strategic position, with a rather different strategic perspective. Where did this come from? Not from any planning process of senior management—in fact, it came as a surprise to that management, even to the filmmakers responsible for it.

A single film ran too long, and not being able to distribute it in the NFB's usual ways, it was marketed as a feature film in theaters. Other filmmakers took notice—"Why not me?"—and before long, some were making feature films of their own, thus taking the organization to a new strategy. Talk about a strategy forming without being formulated!

Throughout the almost forty years that we tracked the strategies of the NFB (as patterns in the films that it made), the organization went through remarkably regular cycles of convergence and divergence: about six years of clear strategic focus (for example, in series made for television, with the advent of this medium), followed by about six years without such focus. Interestingly, many of the NFB's most creative successes came in the latter periods. **Strategic focus can sometimes get in the way of creativity in a project organization, by discouraging the pursuit of novel insights.** Of course, **without such focus, there is the alternate danger of strategic drift**—single projects taking the organization off in all directions.

Inspired by these findings, we developed a *grassroots model of strategy formation* (see box). This may be overstated, but perhaps less so than the widely accepted *hothouse model of strategy formulation*.

A GRASSROOTS MODEL OF STRATEGY FORMATION

- **Strategies grow initially like weeds in a garden, they are not cultivated like tomatoes in a hothouse.** In other words, the strategy process can be overmanaged: sometimes it is better to let patterns emerge than to force a premature consistency on an organization. The hothouse, if needed, can come later.
- **These strategies can take root in all kinds of places, wherever people have the capacity to learn and the resources to support that capacity.** Sometimes an individual or team chances upon an opportunity, or makes a mistake that can be serendipitous. The point is that organizations cannot always plan *where* their strategies will emerge, let alone plan the strategies themselves.
- **Such strategies become organizational when they proliferate as a pattern, to pervade the behavior of the organization.** When weeds proliferate, to encompass a whole garden, the conventional plants may look out of place. Likewise, emergent strategies can sometimes displace the existing, deliberate ones. But, of course, what's a weed but a plant that wasn't expected? With a change of outlook, the emergent strategy, like a weed, can become what is valued. (Europeans eat salads of America's most notorious weed, the dandelion.)
- **This process of proliferation may be conscious, and managed, but need not be.** The means by which a strategic pattern works its way through the organization need not be consciously intended, by official managers or even unofficial ones. A pattern may simply spread by collective action (as in the NFB's feature films), much as do weeds. Of course, when such emergent strategies are recognized as valuable, the proliferation of them can be managed deliberately, just as plants can be selectively propagated.
- **To manage this grassroots process is, thus, not to preconceive strategies, but to recognize their emergence and intervene when appropriate.** A destructive weed, once noticed, is best uprooted immediately. But one that may be capable of bearing fruit is worth watching, indeed sometimes even worth building a hothouse around. To manage in this context is, therefore, to create a climate within which a wide variety of strategies can take root and then watch what does come up, without being too quick to cut off what was unexpected. Overall, the management has to sense when to exploit an established crop of strategies, and when to encourage new strains that might displace them.

Managing in the Forms

As described in Chapter 3, managing may be managing. But it does vary in the four forms.

Irrepressible Managing in the Personal Enterprise

Management in the Personal Enterprise is essentially the chief, irrepressibly, the hub around whom everyone and everything revolves. There may be other managers in particular units, but they tend to take their cues from the chief.

Go into an entrepreneurial company, small or large, and watch the boss, likely being watched by everyone else. "Now listen to me slowly," said the founder of a large chain of supermarkets at a meeting of his executive committee. Little restrains the chief in this organization of minimal structure and few standards, sometimes not even operational planning. Some years ago, I asked a manager in a famous retail chain why they were so often out of stock. "Because the founder hates planning," came the reply.

Micromanaging is bad, right? As noted, if you are the big boss, stick to the big stuff and leave the details to others. This advice itself can be bad, especially (but not only) in the Personal Enterprise. **The big picture has to be painted by little brushstrokes, with clues found on the ground**. Hence, managing on the ground need not be micromanaging. **The best entrepreneurs are masters at consolidating operating details into comprehensive strategic visions.** Rather than formulating to implement, they cycle back and forth between concrete actions and conceptual inferences: they *do* in order to *think*, in order to *do*, in order to *think*...

In terms of the model of managing introduced in Chapter 3, while all managers have to manage on all three planes—of information, people, and action—in the Personal Enterprise we can expect to see more activity on the action plane: more doing on the inside and more dealing on the outside, alongside considerable controlling within the organization on the information plane.

As for the conundrums, of greatest concern here are likely to be: (a) the dilemma of delegating: how to delegate when so much of the relevant information can be personal, oral, and privileged? and (b) the clutch of confidence: how to maintain a sufficient level of confidence without crossing over into arrogance?

Managing as Fine-Tuning the Programmed Machine

If the chief is key in the Personal Enterprise, then the structure is key in the Programmed Machine. Here, with the help of staff analysts, the managers—top, middle, and bottom—program the strategies, which tend to remain rather stable. This means that **the managers have to fine-tune their bureaucratic machine, continuously**, especially to avoid disturbances. Since "uncertainty is the biggest enemy," the lid must be kept tight on the conflicts that arise in these structures.

This was crystal clear when I spent a few days with the managers of a large Red Cross refugee camp in Tanzania, on the borders of Rwanda and Burundi, shortly after the atrocities that occurred in those countries. Here was conventional managing in a most unconventional setting. All was eerily calm in the camp, everything remarkably programmed. Because these camps could blow up at a moment's notice, their managers had to be obsessively responsive to the least little spark.[89]

To keep the organization on course, to avoid disturbances, to contain conflict, the managers of the Programmed Machine thus seek to maintain it as closed as possible—whether by a foreman to keep disruptive visitors out of the factory or by a CEO to keep meddling board members at arm's length. Hence the role of controlling, internally, on the information plane, is pivotal.

When disturbances do appear—when the programs don't go according to plan—*management by exception* **comes to the fore.** The managers must bring the organization back on course. Thus, no matter how programmed the rest of the machine, management itself (really in all four forms) has to function as adhocracy—in other words, flexibly and collaboratively.

As for the conundrums, here four are of particular concern: (a) the labyrinth of decomposition: where to find synthesis in a world so decomposed by analysis? (b) the quandary of connecting: how to keep informed when managing by its very own nature removes the manager from the very things being managed? (c) the mysteries of measuring: how to manage something when you can't rely on measuring it? and (d) the riddle of change: how to manage change when there is an overriding need to maintain continuity? And we mustn't forget the clutch of confidence: with so much control up the hierarchy, it's rather easy to slip from confidence into arrogance.

External Managing in the Professional Assembly

Hierarchy takes a different form in the Professional Assembly. As noted, the professionals look up their own hierarchy of status, while the managers look down their hierarchy of authority, to the less professional staff. Thus do they pass each other like ships in the night.

What the managers here do, at every level, is support the professionals more than supervise them. In a hospital, for example, the executive director as well as the medical chiefs are expected to ensure a steady inflow of funding, whether from donors (e.g., for new equipment) or from government departments (e.g., for bigger budgets), while at the same time holding these same influencers at bay, so that the professionals can work with minimal distraction. Faced with governmental officials and board members who don't appreciate the difference between meritocracy and bureaucracy ("Measure those death rates." "Control those workers like I control my truckdrivers."), **managing in the Professional Assembly requires a delicate balancing act of drawing the outside influencers in while keeping them out.**

Delicate balance is also required to deal with the many jurisdictional disputes that arise in these organizations—the conflicts across the categories. Hence, **to manage a Professional Assembly is to recognize the asymmetry of having to advocate out while reconciling**

in. Facing out, the manager is expected to advocate for the whole organization, yet turning around, they have to face many professionals advocating for their own interests.[90]

This brings to the fore the external roles of managing: communicating on the information plane, linking on the people plane, and dealing (especially negotiating) on the action plane. The managers of the Professional Assembly have to link more than lead and deal more than do, while internally, they have to convince more than control and inspire more than empower. Yet an astute capacity to do all this can render these managers highly influential, even though they may lack the power of managers in the other forms.

Two conundrums are central to this managing: (a) the labyrinth of decomposition: where to find synthesis in a place so decomposed by analysis? and (b) the riddle of change: how to manage change when there is the need to maintain continuity?

Engaged Managing in the Project Pioneer

In the three forms of organizations discussed above, the work of managers is rather differentiated from that of nonmanaging. Not here. As we have seen, **managers in the Project Pioneer commonly engage in the project teams, while many of the experts commonly engage in the process of managing**, for example, by creating the precedents that become strategies. To use the term that has become popular of late, **here we find *distributed* managing**—yet another blurring of the conventional categories.

But with power so decentralized to project teams that can drift off in any direction, the senior managers may have to consolidate disparate actions into coherent strategy—to *nudge* the teams toward what seems to be working best. Andy Grove favored this word when writing about his stewardship at Intel: his inclination to coax behavior in a preferred direction.[91] You don't nudge workers in the personal and machine organization so much as *direct* them. And even trying to nudge the skilled people of a professional organization anywhere can be tricky. But **in an organization that pioneers all kinds of projects, nudging is necessary to move forward, collaboratively.**

If *doing* (on the projects themselves) can be a pivotal inside role for the managers of the Project Pioneer, then *linking* and *dealing* are pivotal roles externally. Managers at all levels of the project organization are very much salespeople, as the partners of adhocratic architecture and consulting firms know full well. Since the project work comes and goes, the managers have to smooth out the bumps by ensuring a somewhat steady stream of new projects. Moreover, because networking is so central to the functioning of these organizations, communicating on the information plane, internally as well as externally, takes on special importance here.

Three managerial conundrums are of special significance here: (a) the syndrome of superficiality: how to get in deep when there is so much pressure to get it done; (b) the predicament of planning: how to plan, strategize, just plain think, let alone think ahead, in such a hectic job; and (c) the ambiguity of acting: how to act decisively in a complicated, nuanced world.

To summarize: in the Personal Enterprise, the chief is the heart and soul of the place, while other managers—if there are others—largely respond to him or her. In the Programmed Machine, the managers fine-tune the systems to keep the organization running smoothly, especially by dealing with unexpected disturbances. In the other two forms, where so much power resides with individual professionals or teams of experts, the managers do not control so much as connect, to link people and projects to each other as well as to the outside world, with much of the regular managing distributed.

The Forms for Real

Are these four forms real? Do they exist? What's real? We have been seeing words and figures on paper or screen. They are real, in their own way, even if not part of the "real world." But show me anything in the real world, and I'll show you something that is real and unreal in its own way.

Reality is too big for our little heads. So we use simplifications of reality to deal with it, impressions of reality: ideas, concepts, frames, models, forms, and theories. These help to explain the reality we encounter. Hence, our choice is not between, let's say, theory and reality, so much as between alternate theories of reality. And this pertains to a manager making a decision as much as to you reading this book. Logically, we choose the theory that is most useful under the circumstances—not the best, but the best available—no matter how imperfect it may be. So, if I have been doing my job well, these forms do exist after all, in your head, there to help you understand and design organizations.

I have offered many examples of the forms throughout this discussion. But if you probe into any of them, you will find anomalies. For example, the players in football—the quintessential programmed sport—require considerable training. And there are pockets of adhocracy in any bureaucracy (try the advertising department), just as there are pockets of bureaucracy in the most creative adhocracy (someone has to staff the mail room). Doctors Without Borders assembles professional hospitals as projects in disaster zones, while TV soap operas sometimes look as programmed as cars coming off an assembly line.

With all these anomalies, should we reject the four forms after all? Not at all, because anomalies are not only real, but common. No organization can be a perfect match for any one form, although quite a few come remarkably close. So far, much of this book has been about them—it has been doing its own pigeonholing. Here, however, we reach a turning point: what follows takes us past the four forms, to open up our discussion.

PART IV

SEVEN BASIC FORCES FOR ORGANIZING

Sometimes it makes more sense to view organizations as a system of forces instead of a portfolio of forms. A number of salient forces pervade organizations. We need to understand them if we are to understand why organizations structure themselves as they do. Chapter 12 describes the force that prevails in each of the four forms, and Chapter 13 introduces three additional forces that can play significant roles in all four forms.

A Force for Each Form

For every form there is a prevalent force: consolidation in the personal organization and collaboration in the project organization, efficiency in the machine organization and proficiency in the professional organization. Each of these forces is described here, briefly, because they have already entered the discussion of the four chapters on the forms.

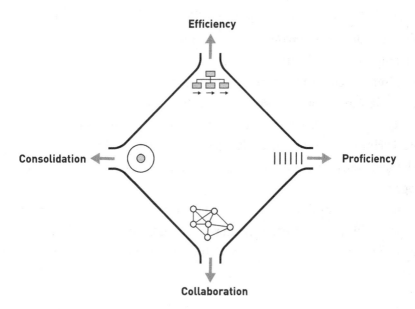

Consolidation in the Personal Enterprise

Usually, the Personal Enterprise has its act together. With its power so concentrated, one person can consolidate the efforts of everyone else.

Moreover, when another form of organization is in crisis, and really does have to get its act together—for example, a machine organization facing bankruptcy—the tendency is to turn to a leader who can best conceive and consolidate the necessary changes. Systems that normally do the consolidating in the machine organization are inadequate under conditions of crisis, and so it may have to revert to a Personal Enterprise for as long as it takes to turn it around. The professional organization, in contrast, usually has little need for consolidation, given that the professionals work rather independently of each other. The project organization may have that need, but normally the networks that connect the projects do that. But in crisis, even the professional and project forms may have to revert to the personal form, however reluctantly, for greater consolidation.

Efficiency in the Programmed Machine

"We need more order around here." This is the mantra of the machine organization, no matter how much order it already has. Order here usually means efficiency—more output bang for the input buck—to minimize its use of resources, including those human resources. **If an organization is organized like a machine, it will focus on efficiency. If, organized differently, it has greater need for efficiency, it will be inclined to reorganize toward the machine form.** Either way, the technostructure will plan more activities, impose more measures, tighten the rules.

But within limits. As noted, the Project Pioneer gets its effectiveness by being *inefficient*, while in the Professional Assembly, efficiency can be the nemesis of proficiency. The Personal Enterprise can usually be made more efficient, but will the chief tolerate all those analysts meddling with his or her organization?

Proficiency in the Professional Assembly

Sheer proficiency is what we look for in our professional organizations—a deft hip replacement, the best meal in town, the perfect double play. Not machine-like efficiency (the most hip replacements/day), not creative collaboration (a novel hip replacement), not consolidation (linking that hip replacement with the heart transplant next door), but empowering the professionals to be as proficient in their work as they can possibly be.

Collaboration in the Project Pioneer

Collaboration is the favored force in the Project Pioneer, to foster innovation. People usually have to work closely together to come up with novel, customized solutions. Sure, these organizations may need consolidation of their projects. But their natural propensity to network can facilitate that. The members of the project teams certainly need to be proficient, but collaboratively, not independently. As for efficiency, while some is always needed, it hardly encourages innovation.

To conclude: what came first, the force or the form? Well, we need an egg to make a chicken and a chicken to make an egg. Here, too, **the force encourages the form and the form gives license to the force.** Together they reinforce each other.

CHAPTER 13

Three Forces for All the Forms

Beside the force for each of the four forms are three more forces for all four of the forms, catalytic in nature. **One of them, *the infusion of culture*, tightens up the structure, by encouraging people to pull together, and the other two loosen it up, the *overlay of separation* by pushing the units away from each other, and the *intrusion of conflict* that pulls people and units apart from each other.** As shown in Figure 13.1, separation is overlaid from above, culture permeates throughout, and conflict acts as a kind of underhand.

The Overlay of Separation (Pushing Away)

Part II of this book described the division of labor, namely how positions in the organization need to be differentiated—separated from each other—and then how they need to connect by the various mechanisms of coordination. Then, in Chapter 5, we discussed unit grouping, whereby these positions are combined into units that are separated from each other by the silos and the slabs, and hence require being brought together by various lateral linkages, systems of planning and control, and the like.

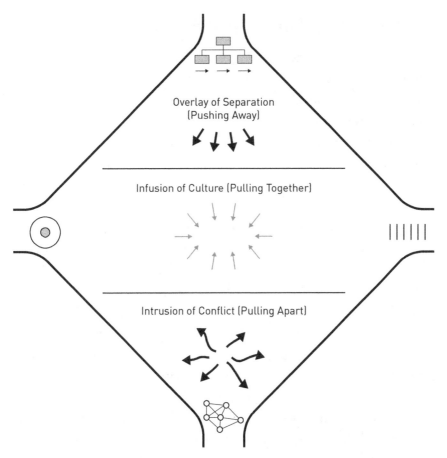

FIGURE 13.1 Three Forces for All the Forms

But **sometimes there is the need to encourage further sepa-ration—to grant units greater autonomy within the structure.** To do this, the organization turns to a loose mechanism of coordination, the standardization of outputs: power to make many decisions is del-egated to these units, subject to achieving the results imposed by the central management. This is the *overlay* of separation—laying sepa-rations over the existing structure. A telephone company that offers land lines, mobile services, and internet connectivity may be inclined to establish a separate division to deal with each.

The Infusion of Culture (Pulling Together)

As discussed in Chapter 2, every organization has a culture, its way of doing things. A research lab just doesn't feel like a bank, or, for that matter, sometimes even one research lab from another. If grouping is the skeleton 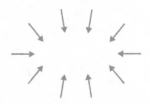 of the organization and systems are its flesh and flows, then culture can be its spirit. *Can be*, because some cultures are ordinary, indistinct, like several supermarket chains where I live. (They can be described as having an industry culture. Likewise, there are occupational cultures, such as in engineering, and, of course, nations are often described as having their own cultures—say, German compared with Italian.)

Organizations with indistinct cultures are like people with indistinct personalities—they are more flesh and bones than heart and soul. But some organizations are distinct: they have their unique ways of doing things. This can render their culture compelling, thus infusing their structure with soul, much as a dye infuses a clear liquid with color. The story is told of three bricklayers. When asked what they do, one says that he is laying bricks, a second that he is building a church, the third that he is creating a monument to the almighty. It is in the third where **the people pull together, as *members* of a community** more than just employees who go to work. **We can call this collective spirit** *communityship*—a word we can use to get past our fixation on leadership.[92] For example:

> Bees and ants are unable to survive in isolation, but in great numbers they act almost like the cells of a complex organism with a collective intelligence and capabilities for adaptation far superior to those of its individual members.[93]

Synergy is a word for this phenomenon, the 2 + 2 = 5 concept: that the parts together produce more than they would apart. **Organizations generally function more effectively when people work in compelling cultures that reduce their status differences.** Whether

THE ENGAGING ORGANIZATION
BY WARREN NILSSON AND TANA PADDOCK

People who are engaged with their organizations describe how alive they feel, how creative and emboldened. They talk about how much they've grown through their work and how much they look forward to entering the organization each day, even when things are difficult or stressful. Here we list six of the most powerful practices that we have seen within engaging organizations.

Organization	→	Engaging Organization
Professional development	→	**Personal growth**
How can we support our career goals?		How can we support our life aspirations?
Roles	→	**Gifts**
What functions do we fill?		What strengths, passions, and curiosities do we bring?
Managing people	→	**Managing relationships**
How do we get the right people?		How do we get the relationships right?
Mission	→	**Purpose**
What is our goal and how do we achieve it?		What is our meaning and how do we live it?
• A mission is expressed in words; it is something to be understood. • A mission can be pursued. • A mission is an answer. • A mission is driven by organizational goals.		• A purpose is experiential; it is something to be lived. • A purpose has to be explored. • A purpose is a question. • A purpose is nurtured by values that are bigger than the organization.
Unified message	→	**Distributed voice**
What are the right words and who are the appropriate people to say them?		How can each of us express our experiences of the organization in our own ways?
Reciprocal exchange	→	**Co-creation**
What do we want from you and what do you want from us?		How can we imagine and build together in line with our purpose?

Source: Excerpted from the CoachingOurselves.org module titled: *Engagement: Beyond Buy-in*

you are sweeping the floors or managing the office, you are recognized for doing your part to make the organization great. See "The Engaging Organization" box to appreciate how compelling cultures work.

While people of other organizations may look outward to what comparable ones are doing, the people in these organizations look inward to the enthusiastic pursuit of its own mission. This could explain why some sports teams with no star players come out of nowhere to win championships. The regular players just played together with exceptional energy: $2 + 2 = 5$. Money can buy stars, but it can't buy conviction. Likewise, sometimes we walk into a hotel or a school and the place just feels different. The people are attentive, responsive, and energized; they serve well because they themselves are respected by their own management (see "A Tale of Two Hotels" box below).

A TALE OF TWO HOTELS

There is a hotel in the north of England that I have been obliged to stay at from time to time—a corporate place with little spirit. I recall a high turnover of staff, and one time, back in the days of landlines, when they charged ten dollars per minute for calls to Japan that cost them about a penny. On one occasion, I left that hotel to check out another one in the English Lake District, for our management program. The minute I entered that hotel, I could feel the energy of the place. It was loaded with soul: beautifully appointed, perfectly cared for, with a genuinely attentive staff (a real smile instead of some grin from a "greeter").

What does it mean for an organization to have a soul? You know it when you see it; you feel it in every detail. I asked a waiter about hiking trails nearby. He didn't know so he fetched the manager, who came right over to tell me, in detail. I asked a young woman at reception how long she had been here. Four years, she said proudly, and then rattled off the tenures of the senior staff: the manager fourteen years, the assistant manager twelve years, the head of sales almost as long.

Most people—employees, managers, customers—want to care, given half a chance. If we human beings have souls, why can't our hotels, hospitals, and schools, let alone our banks and phone companies?

The Development of a Compelling Culture

There are three stages in the development of a compelling culture: founding, diffusing, and reinforcing.

Stage 1: Founding with a sense of mission, often around a charismatic leader, who creates something special, exciting. This is much easier to do in a new organization, unconstrained by procedures and traditions, when people are able to develop close personal relationships—to pull together. In contrast, doing so in an existing organization, with the beliefs and procedures already established, is far more difficult, although sometimes a major event—the arrival of a charismatic leader, a crisis demanding major change—can enable the organization to suspend its usual ways and build culture anew.

Stage 2: Diffusing the beliefs through precedents and stories. As the members collaborate in making decisions and taking actions, precedents are established that can become traditions. Stories are told about inspiring events; the best of which become *sagas,* to use the Nordic label, and these combine to establish a unique history. Gradually the organization gets *infused with value*, to use Philip Selznick's celebrated expression, to become what he called an *institution*, a system with a life of its own, having "acquire[d] a self, a distinct identity."[94]

Stage 3: Reinforcing of the culture through identifications and socialization. People joining such an organization do not enter a random collection of individuals, but a living system, with its traditions and stories. To remain, they must come to identify with all this—become loyal members. Such organizations use interpersonal processes of *socialization*, or *indoctrination*, to institutionalize the commitment of its new members, as well as to reinforce that of the existing ones—for example, with social events of various kinds.

This is how a compelling culture is built—slowly, patiently. Once done, however, it can be difficult to change. But not to kill. Just go back to those "Five Easy Steps to Fix Your Organization" (in Chapter 8), each anathema to compelling culture.

Compelling Cultures in the Four Forms

A compelling culture can infuse any of the four forms, although it comes more readily to some than to others. Many Personal Enterprises fit Stage 1 rather well and so can be on their way to compelling cultures. An entrepreneur pursues a unique vision, which attracts people whom he or she sees as family, and so goes to great lengths to avoid laying them off in a crisis. Of course, once that founder goes, all this can come to an abrupt end.

Programmed Machines tend to be quite the opposite. Standards and systems, rules and measures hardly encourage people to pull together with conviction. Yet compelling cultures can sometimes be found here, too, in what can be called a *snappy bureaucracy*. There is spirit in its flesh, energy in its bones. Colin Hales has called this *"bureaucracy-lite*, not a radical shift to network organization but more limited change to a different form of bureaucracy in which hierarchy and rules have been retained but in an attenuated and sharper form."[95]

In the Professional Assembly, the identifications tend to be individual and professional more than organizational. But given the missions of some of these assemblies—treating the ill, educating children— compelling cultures are not uncommon. In the Project Pioneer, there is more reason to expect compelling culture, thanks to the collaborative spirit that can exist in its teams. The decentralization of authority can help too, but this also allows people to speak their minds which can, as in the Professional Assembly, beget conflict.

The Intrusion of Conflict (Pulling Apart)

"Jobs fall into two classes, My Jobs and Your Jobs. My Jobs are public-spirited proposals, which happen (much to my regret) to involve the advancement of a personal friend, or (still more to my regret) of myself. Your Jobs are insidious intrigues for the advancement of yourself and your friends, speciously disguised as public-spirited proposals."[96]

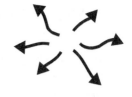

My Oxford dictionary defines *conflict* as "serious disagreement" and *politics* as "activities concerned with gaining or using power within an organization or group." These two terms go together: disagreements arise when different actors try to gain or use power. Hence both will be used here.

Every organization experiences conflict, more or less, even if this is just some clash of personalities. Usually this is limited so that people can get on with things, but not always. Buy a condo and attend the owners' meetings. One group may be determined to spruce up the place to increase its market value while another may be insistent on minimizing the fees. They may simply argue, but in some condos, this becomes cold war.

If a compelling culture pulls people together in an organization (centripetal), then the clashes of conflict pull them apart (centrifugal). Indeed, conflict itself can take a compelling culture apart, just as a compelling culture can bring conflicting parties together. This is a bit like that game where scissors cut paper, rocks crush scissors, and paper covers rocks.

For people trying to get things done in an organization, conflict and politics can feel intrusive. After all, if organizing is about attaining order, conflict is disorderly. But in the larger scheme of things, conflict is as natural as culture. Once again, even bees do it (see box).

POLITICS IN A BEEHIVE

Various messenger bees go out to find fields of flowers, or a new site for their hive, and on return, do dances that demonstrate the qualities of the finds. The bees decide collectively which is best, and in the case of a new hive, swarm that way. (These bees are more democratic than we humans!) Once, however, a researcher was astonished by what he saw:

> Two groups of messengers had got into competition; one group announced a nesting place to the northwest, the other to the northeast. Neither of the two wished to yield. The swarm finally flew off and I could scarcely believe my eyes—it sought to divide itself....Apparently each group of scouting bees wanted to abduct the swarm to the nesting place of its choice. But that was not naturally possible, for one group was always without the queen, and there resulted a remarkable tug of war in the air, once 100 meters to the northwest, then again 150 meters to the northeast, until finally after half an hour the swarm gathered at the old location. Immediately both groups began with their soliciting dances, and it was not until the next day that the northeast group finally yielded; they ended their dances and thus an agreement was reached on the nesting place in the northwest.[97]

Like bees, we are naturally collaborative creatures who can be highly competitive. Our cultures pull us together and our conflicts pull us apart. When we disagree, we might "play politics," meaning acting underhandedly, outside the formal structure. If this sounds like some sort of game, it can, in fact, be seen as a whole set of them, some of which challenge the legitimate power of authority, expertise, culture, or else break down formal structure, while others use some legitimate kind of power in illegitimate ways.

Political Games in Organizations

Here are thirteen of the most common political games played in organizations.[98]

- **The insurgency game** is usually played to resist authority in an organization, although it can also be used to resist expertise or established culture, also to effect change. And so it tends to be played by people in weaker positions who feel the full weight of some form of legitimate power.

- **The counterinsurgency game** is played by those with legitimate power who fight back insurgencies with political actions, or legitimate actions used politically (as in the use of excommunication in a church to punish a dissenter).

- **The sponsorship game** is played by using someone in a more senior position to build a power base: an individual attaches him- or herself to a person with more status, professing loyalty in return for influence.

- **The alliance-building game** is played among peers, often line managers, sometimes staff experts, who negotiate implicit contracts of support for each other to advance their interests in the organization.

- **The empire-building game** is played especially by line managers, to build power bases, not cooperatively but personally, by maneuvering to enlarge their units.

- **The budgeting game** is played overtly and with rather clearly defined rules, to increase budgets. It is similar to the last game but is less divisive, since the prize is resources, not people. A common version of this game is to spend remaining funds on something not particularly necessary before they run out.

- **The expertise game** flaunts or feigns expertise. True experts flaunt the uniqueness and irreplaceability of their skills and knowledge, also resist having their skills programmed by keeping their knowledge to themselves. Nonexperts feign expertise, or else try to have their work viewed as expert, ideally to have it declared professional so that they can control it.

- **The lording game** is played by lording legitimate power over those without it, or with less of it. A manager lords formal authority over a member of his or her unit; a civil servant lords control of the rules over a citizen; an expert lords his or her technical skills over the unskilled.

- **The line versus staff game**, of sibling-type rivalry, is played, not just to enhance personal power, but also to defeat rivals. It pits line managers with formal authority against staff advisers with specialized expertise, each prepared to exploit legitimate power illegitimately.

- **The rival camps game** is also played to defeat rivals. Two camps form in the organization and challenge each other. This can occur when alliance- or empire-building games end with two major power blocs that fight it out. Being zero-sum, this can be the most divisive game of all, akin to civil war. The conflict can be between units (for example, engineering versus architecture on a building site), between rival personalities (two executives vying to become CEO), even between two competing missions (as in prisons split between staff favoring custody and rehabilitation).

- **The strategic candidate game** is played by individuals or groups determined to promote a favored strategic option through the use of political means. Possible players of this game can include analysts, operators, and managers, even chief executives. (A number of the other games are played within this one.)

- **The whistle blowing game,** typically brief and simple, is also played to effect change in the organization, but of a different kind. An insider, usually not senior, uses restricted information to blow the whistle on some questionable or illegal behavior within the organization, by informing influential outsiders, or some senior insider, even a member of the board of directors. This game is often stymied by the guilty party, in a version of the counterinsurgency game.

- **The subversion game** is played for the highest stakes of all, not just to effect simple change or resist legitimate authority, but to throw the latter into question, perhaps even overthrow it. A small group of determined insiders, sometimes close but not quite at the center of power, seeks to alter the organization's strategy, change its culture, or replace its leadership.

Some of these political games, such as sponsorship, lording, budgeting, and line versus staff, while themselves technically illegitimate, *coexist* with legitimate systems of influence; indeed, they could not exist without them. Other political games, such as insurgency and subversion, arise in the presence of legitimate power but are *antagonistic* to it.

Conflict in the Four Forms

The least amount of conflict might be expected in the Personal Enterprise, where a chief who is in close touch with everything can snuff it out quickly. Of course, if the chief falters, look for the insurgency or subversion game to force him or her out. But even that can be tricky. Witness all those autocrats who have hung on to power long after their time was due, thanks to their control of the levers of power—the armed forces for dictators, sycophants for company chiefs.

In the Programmed Machine, the sharp divisions of labor, and resulting silos and slabs, encourage parochialism that gives rise to political games intended to build narrow bases of power—empire building, budgeting, sponsorship, line versus staff. And while the tight controls may discourage the more antagonistic political games, look especially for the lording game, sometimes also insurgency, subversion, and whistle blowing.

The professional and project organizations have weaker systems of authority but stronger systems of expertise, the powers of which are widely dispersed. Thus, look for considerable political activity here, especially the games that pit groups of insiders against each other, whether to enhance narrow bases of power or just to battle with rivals. Professional Assemblies are especially inclined to split into rival camps on ideological grounds, while the strategic candidates game can be common in the Project Pioneer.

Constructive Conflict

Little space need be devoted to the divisive and costly role of conflict in organizations: we know how much useful energy can be wasted in playing these political games. What does deserve space, however, because it is less widely appreciated, is how conflict and especially politics can be constructive.

In general, politics can be necessary to correct certain deficiencies in an organization's legitimate systems of influence. Put differently, politics, whose *means* are (by definition) illegitimate, can be used to pursue *ends* that are legitimate—as when a whistleblower reveals the abusive behavior of a boss. We can elaborate on this in two specific points.

First, politics as a system of influence can act in a Darwinian way to ensure that the strongest members of an organization are brought into positions of leadership. Because authority favors a single chain of command, weak leaders can suppress strong subordinates. Politics, on the other hand, can provide alternate channels of communication and promotion, as when the sponsorship game enables someone to leap over a weak boss. Moreover, since dealing with conflict is a key part of the manager's job, the political games can demonstrate a person's potential for leadership. The second-string players may suffice for the scrimmages, but better to have the best meeting the competition. Political games not only suggest who these players are, but also help to remove their weaker rivals from contention.

Second, politics can promote different sides of an issue when the legitimate systems of influence promote only one. It can thus force an organization to face changes that have been resisted by its vested interests—the whistle-blowing game being a clear use of this.

The system of authority, by aggregating information up the hierarchy, tends to advance a single point of view, often the one already known to be favored by the people in authority. The system of expertise can concentrate power in the hands of established experts, with their entrenched paradigms and protocols, while a compelling culture is rooted in firmly established beliefs. In the face of all these obstacles, politics can work as an "invisible hand"—more to the point, an *underhand*—to promote necessary change, through such games as strategic candidates, whistle blowing, and subversion. (Other benefits of politics will be discussed in Chapter 16, about the Political Arena, where politics engulf an organization.)

Obviously, political confrontation does not always correct a bad situation. Sometimes it exacerbates it, the solution proving worse than the problem. Moreover, some political challenges are arbitrary, or neutral: an influencer, for example, simply wants a new deal. In these cases, we cannot call politics constructive or destructive, although the period during which it endures can be called dysfunctional, since it uses resources that could have been doing other things. Hence the sooner the politics abate, the better.

Culture and Conflict

Culture and conflict coexist in organizations, sometimes to challenge each other—pulling together versus pulling apart—but also to keep each other in check. As shown in Figures 13.2a and b, **a culture of inclusiveness can constrain the intrusiveness of conflict, just as the intrusiveness of conflict can loosen a culture that has become too inclusive.**

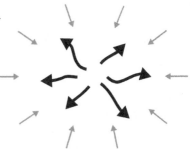

FIGURE 13.2a

Culture to Contain Conflict

Again, the arrows can tell the story. As various actors pursue their

self-interest, the centrifugal force of
conflict that could explode an organization can be restrained by the
centripetal force of culture. Consider, for example, those Project
Pioneers whose experts challenge
each other internally yet present
a united front externally once they
have made their decisions. Likewise,
a culture of overworked beliefs that
is imploding can be pulled open by

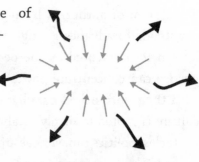

FIGURE 13.2b
Conflict to Open Culture

the explosive force of conflict. Hence **the dynamic balance necessary
in organizations can be maintained by the tension between culture
and conflict.**

PART V

THREE MORE FORMS

If each of the four forms has a corresponding force, then each of these three additional forces can have a corresponding form, where it is predominant. When the autonomy of separation dominates, we find a Divisional Form (Chapter 14); when compelling culture dominates, we find a Community Ship (Chapter 15); and when it is conflict that dominates, we find a Political Arena (Chapter 16).

These three forms may be less fundamental than the other four, but we need to understand them nonetheless. The Divisional Form, while quite common, tends to be an extension of the Programmed Machine. The Community Ship is less common, yet examples show how striking can be its significance. So too the Political Arena, a form that tends to be temporary because it can be so extreme.

CHAPTER 14

The Divisional Form

Let's say you make canoes in Canada. Why not kayaks? Expand your market with many of the same materials, processes, and customers. Well, then, why not paddles? Different materials but the same customers. And how about docks? After all, some of these customers buy docks. Next thing you know, you're making icebreakers. Uh oh!

This is the road to *diversification*—from different products to different businesses—taken not only by many companies but also by organizations in the plural and public sectors. **Diversification starts with** *related* **products or services** (kayaks after canoes) **and ends with ones that are** *unrelated* (ice breakers) **in what is called a** *conglomerate*. For years, big business, especially in America, has gone through waves of conglomeration followed by consolidation (as we shall discuss).

Diversification leads to *divisionalization*: **a company operating in separate businesses creates separate units—usually called** *divisions*—**to deal with each, subject to oversight (in both senses, as we shall see) by a headquarters that controls them through the enforcement of standards of performance.** How much autonomy they get depends on how different they are from each other: we might expect the icebreaker division to have more autonomy than the kayak division.

Here, then, we have the Divisional Form, also called *federation* in some nations and NGOs. Canada is a federation of provinces, for instance, and the International Federation of Red Cross and Red Crescent Societies has almost two hundred branches in countries around the world.[99] Since the Divisional Form has been most widely used in business, much of the discussion that follows will rely on business examples and experience, until we come to the final section of the chapter, which considers its use in these other sectors.

Expanding Out, Acquiring In

Diversification is associated with growth and aging. As an organization grows, it may run out of opportunities to expand in its traditional business, and as it ages, its managers may seek opportunities beyond the established business. It is thus hardly coincidental that **so many large established corporations end up with some variant of the Divisional Form**.

From canoes to kayaks is an example of a company *expanding out*— by developing from one business to another. When a company does a great deal of this, we might refer to it as engaging in *crystalline diversification*, since it grows like a crystal, as did 3M in the US (from sandpaper to all sorts of bonding and coating products) and Panasonic in Japan (which began with lightbulb sockets and now produces a wide range of consumer electronics). With their steady stream of innovations, these companies can also be seen as Project Pioneers.

If an organization can expand out, it can also acquire in, by purchasing other companies. Sometimes this is referred to as a *merger*, although many such "mergers" amount to acquisitions, as the bigger company gobbles up the smaller one.

Acquisitions that happen within the same industry—say, when one brewery acquires another—are normally thought of as *related diversification*. With regard to strategy maybe, but **with regard to structure, there is no such thing as a related acquisition.** The very next day, the only thing those two breweries have in common is the thought that they both brew beer. They have no brands in common, no brewing in common, no managers in common, no culture in common (in their beers as well as in their structures). These have to be grown together, consolidated, and that may be easier for the cultures of their beers than for the cultures of their organizations. It can take years to get the people to function together harmoniously. And when they really do merge, as relative equals, this can be more difficult still, because there is no one authority to force them to cooperate: no queen CEO, so to speak (see box, of a story told to me by a beekeeper).

HOW TO MERGE?

When a beekeeper wishes to combine two colonies of bees, the first thing to be done is to remove one of the queen bees several days in advance, to avoid intense conflict. Then the two colonies are placed separately in a box, with a sheet of newspaper between them that has pinholes. Without this, they will attack each other, but with it, they begin to smell each other out. Gradually, as they bite away at the paper, their scents combine. When the paper is gone, the two colonies merge, apparently sometimes even colonies of different breeds.

The opposite can be seen with internal diversification. Much as a child gradually grows apart from its parents, yet never completely, so too a business tends to remain connected to the others from which it was spun off. After all, it grew out of the same culture.

A brewery can easily add cherry beer to its product line: put in the flavor, print new labels, and market accordingly, most of this with the same employees. But if it wishes to turn this into a Flavored Beer Division—cherry, banana, rosewater, whatever—these activities will have to be grown apart—weaned off the mother beer, so to speak. Yet the bond never quite breaks, because the personal relationships remain. Betty in banana beer can call her old buddy at headquarters: "Hey Bruce, can you help me with this problem?" whereas Arthur in the acquired beer company has no buddy at HQ.

Stages in the Transition to the Divisional Form

In business the transition to the Divisional Form is commonly described in four stages.[100]

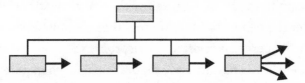

- **Stage 1: Vertical Integration.** Let's start with a company that is fully integrated along its chain of operations—say, from purchasing to production to marketing to sales—with coordination between these managed centrally, through the standardization of work and outputs. In this first stage, known as vertical integration (although, typically shown horizontally, along the operating chain), the company acquires other companies, or develops these activities internally, at either end of its operations. Our canoe company buys a manufacturer of Kevlar, or a chain of sporting goods stores. There may be a need to integrate the different cultures, but otherwise the structure remains functionally integrated.

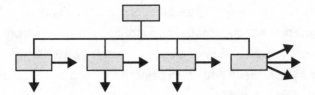

- **Stage 2: By-Product Diversification.** As an integrated company seeks wider markets, it may decide to sell its intermediate products on the open market, in what is called by-product diversification. The canoe department might sell its yokes to other canoe companies. Similarly, an aluminum company could be selling by-product chemicals from its refining process or even excess cargo space in its transport vehicles. This introduces breaks in the operating chain—now the sales people who were selling canoes or aluminum ingot have to sell yokes or chemicals and space to new customers—but otherwise the structure remains intact.

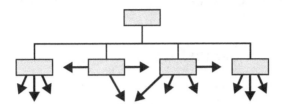

- **Stage 3: Related-Product Diversification.** The next stage begins when the by-products sales become as important as those of the original products. Now our canoe company finds itself seriously in the yoke business, and so dedicates a division to doing that, with somewhat greater autonomy.

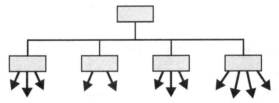

- **Stage 4: Conglomerate Diversification.** The final stage occurs when the differentiation of products and services is rather complete: our company makes icebreakers that have nothing to do with canoes (except in some managerial mind that both are boats). Hence the divisions can be run as full-fledged businesses in their own right. Hydro Quebec, for instance, established a consulting division to offer its world-class engineering capabilities to power companies abroad.

So far, this discussion has concentrated on the diversification of products and services. But **companies can also diversify their customers as well as their regions of operation**—for example, selling the canoes to summer camps or to hotels in the English Lake District. This amounts to a more limited form of diversification because, with identical products for all customers or regions, the headquarters is inclined to keep central control of certain critical functions—say, the design of the canoes, if not the selling of them—thus maintaining some aspects of the integrated structure. Just have a look at the stores of a global retail chain.

The Basic Divisional Structure

True divisions function with considerable autonomy, from each other as well as from the central headquarters, subject mainly to the performance controls of analysts at that headquarters. They set the targets and monitor the results. These controls are not supposed to be intrusive—the division managers are supposed to run their own businesses—but they can become so when the measures keep ratcheting up.

Some important roles do, however, always remain at the headquarters: (1) managing the portfolio of divisions (namely which ones to add, keep, close, or sell); (2) appointing and, when necessary, replacing the division managers; (3) moving the funds around the divisions, to favor those perceived to have the greatest potential for growth while drawing funds out of those that don't (sometimes called "cash cows"); and (4) providing certain support services for all the divisions, such as legal counsel and government relations. As O'Toole and Bennis have written about the federal structure, "The central authority establishes the why and the what; the units are responsible for the how."[101] Does all this constitute decentralization (see box)?

IS DIVISIONALIZATION DECENTRALIZATION?

The prevalent answer to this question has been yes. It is not the correct one.

The Divisional Form rose to prominence early in the twentieth century. As large businesses that were structured functionally began to diversify, they ran into difficulties trying to coordinate the functions across the different businesses (sales for canoes and icebreakers). Restructuring toward the Divisional Form could enable the managers of these businesses to focus on their own functions. But does this constitute decentralization? Compared with keeping most of the decision-making power at headquarters, perhaps. But what if the power delegated to the divisions remains mainly with their own senior management? A few managers with the lion's share of the power in an organization of thousands of people hardly constitutes decentralization. In the labels introduced in Chapter 5, **divisionalization may result in a rather limited form of vertical decentralization**: down the hierarchy one level.

This was evident in the most famous example of divisionalization, mistakenly labeled decentralization. William C. Durant stitched together a number of independent automobile companies—Chevrolet, Buick, Cadillac, and so on—to create General Motors, with almost no central staff. When Alfred Sloan took over in 1923, recognizing the need to rein in the heads of these businesses, he instituted a divisional structure with financial control at the headquarters. In other words, Sloan did not decentralize General Motors: relatively speaking, he *centralized* it. But the word has often been misused ever since. (How ironic that while the Divisional Form came to be called *decentralized* in America, the Communist countries of Eastern Europe, that used a similar structure to control their state-owned companies, came to be called *centralized* in the West.)

The Divisions Driven to the Programmed Machine

In principle, the divisions themselves can take on any structural form. In practice, one form tends to be favored over the others.

Imagine if McDonald's acquired Amazon. Don't hold your breath, but if it did, no matter how different their businesses, with both companies being rather machine-like, that combination could conceivably work. Now imagine, instead, if McDonald's acquired Apple. This would not be a happy union, especially for all those Apple engineers whose idea of innovation is not an Egg McMuffin. A Project Pioneer cannot function effectively under the control of a Programmed

Machine, with headquarters' analysts descending on these engineers in search of efficiency at the expense of creativity. They needs slack, not a straightjacket.

One conclusion in Chapter 6 was that the greater the external control of an organization, the more centralized and formalized its structure, these being the prime characteristics of the machine organization (as was elaborated in Chapter 8). The standards tend to formalize the structure of the divisions, and holding their chiefs responsible for meeting these standards tends to centralize them. Therefore **the Divisional Form is inclined to drive its divisions toward the machine form**, even when they require a different one. For example, the ups and downs associated with project work can be anathema to a headquarters that expects steady increases in performance.

Shortly after Jack Welch became CEO of General Electric, one of his advisers, who had read an early version of this book, called me with a question: What to do with the GE divisions that were more like adhocracies—say, the maker of jet engines compared with light bulbs. Keep the headquarters technocrats at bay, I suggested, by designating these divisions as Welch's own preserves. In effect, use a personal structure at HQ to protect those divisions.

This was illustrated poignantly in another experience I had, with a British company called Thorn EMI, a conglomerate that combined Jules Thorn's original lighting business with the EMI Music company and another business. An executive there told me that "since Thorn died, nobody knows how to run this place." Thorn would seem to have run it, not as a classic Divisional Form, but as his Personal Enterprise. **Could it be that the only way to run a conglomerate successfully, for a time at least, is to have an astute CEO who picks the right businesses and the right people to manage them?**

The Cons of Conglomeration

The conglomerates of business do not have a happy record, at least in the United States. These have come and gone in waves, frequently put together by successful entrepreneurs who diversified companies that eventually collapsed.

Why, then, do conglomerates keep coming back into fashion, time after time? Perhaps because **too many successful companies run out of high-growth opportunities in their own business, but not out of executives who believe they can manage any business, driven by stock market analysts clamoring for steadily greater growth.** After all, there have been no shortage of investors willing to go with superstar successes, such as a Google, or a Beatrice Foods that ended up with four hundred businesses, many in its earlier dairy industry but others in car rentals, luggage, and more, before all that collapsed. If Beatrice had been so good at milking one business, why not four hundred of them, and the me-too investors in the bargain?

There have been exceptions, such as a GE that pulled off conglomeration for quite a while before it consolidated. And conglomerates have sometimes fared better in other parts of the world, especially Asia. For example, Tata of India has been successful with an extraordinary array of businesses. Could this be because control of its voting shares has remained with a set of family trusts that keep the stock market analysts at bay? Or that its most successful CEO was skilled at picking heads of the different businesses, to whom he gave substantial independence, while socializing them carefully into the Tata culture?[102]

The conglomerate has usually been compared to the single, functionally structured business. But from the point of view of economic development, perhaps it should be compared with a set of independent businesses, each with its own board of directors and owners. Here are some of the pros and cons.

1. **The efficient allocation of capital.** On the one hand, it has been claimed that a headquarters can know its businesses better and move money between them faster. On the other hand, it has been claimed that investors can diversify their portfolios cheaper and

quicker (bearing in mind that conglomerates can pay a premium for the businesses they acquire).

2. **The training of general managers.** By running their own businesses, the division heads can develop their managerial skills. But if autonomy is so good for developing managers, might not more autonomy be better? The division managers have a headquarters to lean on, and be leaned on by, whereas independent CEOs might learn better from their own mistakes. One prominent self-proclaimed "deconglomerater" ended up "selling divisions back to their managers. The reason is obvious. The managers know what they are doing."[103]

3. **The spreading of risk.** Operating in different businesses spreads the risk, compared with having all the eggs in one business. But the risk can spread the other way too—for example, when a nuclear power division signs a disastrous contract for uranium that bankrupts the entire conglomerate. Moreover, conglomeration can conceal a de facto bankruptcy when the HQ believes it can turn a failing business around, whereas market forces may be able to rid the economy of independent failing businesses more quickly.

4. **The enhancement of strategic responsiveness.** Each division can fine tune its individual business while the headquarters can focus on the overall portfolio of businesses. But with relentless pressure from a headquarters for steadily higher performance, the division managers might be discouraged from taking risks that do not pay off quickly, whereas an independent business might be able to find patient capital that allows it to take those risks. "[M]ajor new developments are, with few exceptions, made outside the major firms in the industry. Those exceptions tend to be single-product companies whose top managements are committed to true product leadership.... Instead, the diversified companies give us a steady diet of small incremental change."[104]

To conclude, **the advantages of conglomeration might disappear with rectification of the problems it is claimed to address, such as inefficient capital markets and weak boards of independent companies. Trying to manage a company that does not know what business it is in can amount to** *diversifiction*.[105] Hence, from a social no less than an economic point of view, societies may be better off correcting fundamental inefficiencies in their economic systems than supporting private administrative arrangements to overcome them (see box).

THE SOCIAL PERFORMANCE OF THE PERFORMANCE CONTROL SYSTEM

Measurement of performance counts above all else in the Divisional Form. This may seem objective enough: after all, do the numbers lie?

Yes, often. We all know how to game the numbers, even if we sometimes end up gaming ourselves.[106] Moreover, the numbers often distort.[107] This can have serious consequences for the social performance of organizations that rely on them.

Some years ago, in "A note on that dirty word efficiency," I discussed why the word *efficiency* has developed a bad reputation.[108] (Who looks forward to a visit from an "efficiency expert"?) Two questions help to explain this. First, if I say that a restaurant is *efficient*, what is the first thing that pops into your head? Did you think *speed of service*? Most people do (at least anglophones; the word *efficiency* is used differently in some other languages). Why not the quality of the food? (My father said that if he heard that a restaurant was efficient, he would wonder about the food!)

Second, if I say that my house is efficient, to what do you think this refers? Overwhelmingly, people say the cost of heating. But whoever bought a house because of the cost of heating, compared, say, with its design, or the quality of the local schools?

Do you see what is going on? When we hear the word *efficiency*, we zero in, *subconsciously*, on whatever criterion is most measurable. Speed of service. Cost of heating. Efficiency reduces to *measurable* efficiency, and herein lies the problem, with three important consequences:

1. **Because costs are usually easier to measure than benefits, efficiency often reduces to economy**—namely, cutting measurable costs at the expense of less measurable benefits. Think of all those governments that have cut the costs of health care and education while the unmeasured quality of those services has deteriorated. (To repeat: Can we really measure what a child actually learns in a classroom?) How about those CEOs who cut budgets for research or maintenance so that they can earn bigger bonuses quickly? And don't forget that student in Chapter 1 who found all sorts of ways to make an orchestra more efficient.

2. **Because economic costs are typically easier to measure than social costs, efficiency can exacerbate social problems**. Making a factory or an orchestra or a school more efficient is easy, so long as you don't care about the air, the music, or the minds that are polluted.

3. **Because economic benefits are typically easier to measure than social benefits, efficiency can drive us to an economic mind-set that depreciates quality**. We are efficient when we eat fast food instead of healthier food.

So beware of efficiency, and of efficiency experts, as well as of efficient education, health care, and music, plus any organization enamored with measurement. Be careful about *balanced scorecards* too, however well-intentioned they may be (to give attention to social and other goals beside financial ones).[109] Here, too, the dice are loaded in favor of what best lends itself to measurement. And the next time you hear someone say, "If you can't measure it, you can't manage it," ask them who has ever successfully measured culture, leadership, even management itself. Indeed, who has ever even tried to measure the performance of measurement, instead of assuming that it is a holy grail? Whether or not you can *measure* it, you had better *manage* it.

Everything that businesses, as well as governments and NGOs, do has social as well as economic consequences. The more their managers are controlled by the measures, the greater the likelihood that they will be distracted from the social consequences of their actions. This is how the Divisional Form can drive its managers to be socially unresponsive, if not socially irresponsible. To my mind, this is one of the greatest problems facing our world of organizations today.

The Divisional Form beyond Business

When business adopts some new structure or technique, expect much of government to follow suit. And so it has been with the Divisional Form, including its predisposition to control through measures of performance.

This is encouraged by the fact that **government is the ultimate conglomerate.** Transportation, health care, education, tax collection, and much more all report up one hierarchy, culminating in the government in power. **Even many government departments are conglomerates in their own right**. Consider the Department of Transportation—most every country has one. It sounds fine, but tell me: What do the regulation of trucks on the road, control of airplanes in the air, and patrol of boats at sea have in common, besides the notion in our heads that all are about vehicles that move?

Why do governments create these unnatural units? Perhaps because they have to limit the size of their cabinets. If Transportation was split into three separate departments, each requiring its own minister, and other departments followed suit, cabinets would become unmanageable. Better, apparently, to render the departments of government unmanageable.

What's the head of a Department of Transportation to do when other people manage each of its real parts? When considering an answer, bear in mind that there can be nothing more dangerous in an organization than a manager with nothing to do. That is because most managers are energetic: they will find something to do, like adding new measures of performance, or calling meetings of the heads of disassociated units to exploit synergies where there are none to be found.

The popular fix for the problems of managing government, called the *New Public Management* (meaning the old corporate practices), pours oil on this fire. Let the managers manage the departments, it proclaims, be "accountable" in the popular word, subject to meeting the performance targets imposed by analysts in the central techno-structure. In other words, use the Divisional Form.

But this is no fix at all, for three reasons. First, as noted, the goals of government are significantly social and therefore often not amenable to workable measurement. Quality thus suffers. Second, because the politicians are the ones ultimately accountable, to the public, they often preempt the accountability of the public sector managers. Come some crisis, they can be all over them. And third, while the markets can bring down dysfunctional companies, there is no mechanism to bring down dysfunctional government departments. Hence many just fester.

Consider what excessive performance measuring has done to so much public education—for example, by the use of multiple-choice examinations that violate the imagination of children. Very efficient indeed. As for health care, when a senior civil servant in the UK was asked why his health department measured so much, he replied: "What else can we do when we don't know what's going on?" How about leaving your office, to find out what's going on—for instance, that your measures may be driving the professionals quite literally to distraction?

Much the same can be concluded about the use of the Divisional Form in the plural sector. **Many of the associations in the sector—charities, NGOs, foundations, and so on—serve social needs. This renders their use of the conventional Divisional Form problematic, at least in the conglomerate version where it relies on numerical controls.** Limited forms of diversification—for example, based on geographic region—can work better, as in the Red Cross Federation with its national societies.

Some business schools in the US have opened campuses in other countries and some hospitals have created clones in other cities to leverage their reputation. But is continuing to function under one institutional umbrella preferable to cutting the new places loose once they have become established?

One thing is clear: Governments and associations should no more be run like businesses than should businesses be run like governments and associations.

To conclude, **in its ultimate, conglomerate version, the Divisional Form can be described as a structure on the edge of a cliff. Taking one step ahead, it shatters into pieces on the rocks below. Behind are the safer places of an intermediate form** (related-product, by-product, geographic), with some synergy but less measurement.

CHAPTER 15

The Community Ship

While all organizations are influenced by their culture, or lack of it, some have cultures so compelling to their *members*—who are more than "employees"—that the force of pulling together dominates. **The label Community Ship is used here to suggest that these organizations function as tightly knit communities, quite apart from other organizations, like ships at sea. They can close ranks for protection,** like a herd of muskoxen that form a ring around their calves, **or else use their position for evangelism**, namely to launch missives at whatever they want to change on shore. (We should not, however,

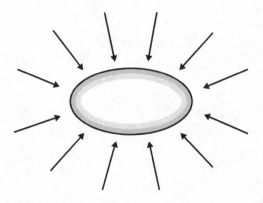

confuse Community Ships with *communities of practice*, where people with some common interest connect to share experience. These are really *networks* of practice.)

The Basic Structure

Organizations with this kind of commitment rely on the standardization of norms for coordination, rather than on direct supervision, mutual adjustment, or some other form of standardization. **The members adhere not to the rules so much as to the "word": the social beliefs of the organization, the gravitational pull of its ideology,** whether to convert the heathens, build windmills to reverse climate change, or win a championship.

Otherwise, the Community Ship is hardly structured at all. Don't look for extensive rules, regulations, systems, and hierarchy here. The Personal Enterprise at least has its chief, formally in charge. In a sense, in a Community Ship, the established culture is in charge. A cluster of members pulls together within that culture, with minimum specialization of jobs, differentiation of parts, and distinctions of status.

As a consequence, **the Community Ship is the most decentralized organization of all, with its power spread more evenly than in any other form.** Once accepted into the fold, everyone is respected, and expected to act for the good of the organization, without much need for controls beyond the standardization of those norms. Paradoxically, however, **the Community Ship is the most controlling of all the forms**, for here the standards capture people's souls, not just direct their efforts.

In the original Israeli kibbutz—village and community wrapped into one—everything was shared, cars and all. Even managerial positions were rotated. No wonder they fared better as Community Ships when they focused on agriculture, with their members planting and harvesting by day and making decisions together in the evening, than when they turned to industry, which required more specialized expertise and more concerted management. To avoid a managerial elite, another Community Ship, the Foundation for Infantile Paralysis, which famously funded the research that led to the Salk Vaccine, did not allow doctors to hold office in its local chapters.[110]

Consider quality. In the machine organization, certain analysts are in charge of "quality control," while in the professional and project organizations, each professional or team is concerned with the quality of their own work—and indeed, can be reluctant to judge the quality of others. In the Community Ship, everyone is concerned with the quality of everything that everyone does.

Here, then, **leadership serves *communityship*.** It is expected to interpret the "word" but not change it. The queen bee in the hive provides an excellent example: "She issues no orders; she obeys, as meekly as the humblest of her subjects...we will term [this] the 'spirit of the hive.'"[111] But by her very presence, manifested in the emitting of a chemical substance, she unites the members of the hive and galvanizes them into action. In a Community Ship, we call this substance culture: it is the spirit of the human hive.

Dedication to mission is maintained in the Community Ship by the careful selection of new members, followed by informal processes of socialization and indoctrination. For example, new recruits to a religious order, also to the traditional Japanese enterprise, go through an extensive period of learning how to behave in the organization. Thereafter, the members don't have to be formally "empowered" because they are naturally engaged, although they are persistently reminded, and remind others, of being "correct" in whatever they do.

Communityship is easier to sustain when the units remain small, because so much of what happens depends on personal contact. Thus, when such an organization grows beyond the size where its members can easily maintain such contact, it tends to divide itself, like an amoeba, not into divisions so much as into self-contained replicas of its initial self, as the Israeli kibbutzim have typically done after reaching a certain size.

A QUINTESSENTIAL COMMUNITY SHIP

Years ago, I visited Myrada in action on several occasions, an Indian NGO whose mission has been "building local people's institutions" in the form of "self-help groups of poor rural women."[112]

Each of our visits was roughly the same, in spirit as well as activity. Just under twenty village women, all dressed in matching saris, sat on the floor in one of their houses, like one—as bonded as any group I have ever seen. A few of us sat on the floor facing them, to listen to what they wished to say. Each time, the energy and enthusiasm of those women, their pride, curiosity, and confidence, was memorable. (Meanwhile, outside, the men were ambling about like a bunch of tomcats, occasionally peering in to see to what was going on.)

They explained how Myrada taught them to self-organize, take action to improve their lives, educate their children, deal with pregnancy, start a small business. In those days, something as simple as learning how to sign their name could enable these women to secure a loan at a bank to buy a cow.

The groups were typically started by one woman who, after receiving training with Myrada, returned home to organize it. Another woman was trained to do the bookkeeping. But always, there was a sense of collective engagement.

After the presentations, we asked questions. Watching one of the women taking profuse notes of one discussion, one of us asked what they would do with those notes. We were told that they would go over each one meticulously in a later meeting. Someone asked how their husbands felt about them leaving the isolation of their homes to meet together. One woman, who had been rather quiet, volunteered that, at first she was scared to attend, but after she had bought a cow and was creating some income for the family, her husband encouraged her to go.

The images of those women sitting there as one has remained vivid in my mind ever since—a wonderful example of Community Ship.

Types of Community Ships

Most everything above suggests that **Community Ships are most likely to be found in the plural sector.** Without the pressures that come from being publicly or privately owned, mission can come to the fore. Hence, we have seen the examples of religious orders, kibbutzim, and the Myrada, although some businesses, even the occasional government agency, do manage to escape the usual controls to pursue belief in an esteemed mission. Mitz Noda has attributed the great success of Japanese corporations post–World War II to "stressing teamwork, group decision-making, lifetime employment, and uniform basic raises and bonuses," thereby encouraging "group effort rather than unilateral leadership."[113]

We can distinguish three types of Community Ships. **The *reformers* seek to change the world directly**, whether to save the climate or overthrow a government. **The *converters* seek to change the members they attract**. Alcoholics Anonymous is a converter, the Women's Christian Temperance Union (that sought to rid the US of alcohol consumption) was a reformer. **The *cloisters* seal themselves off** (e.g., to escape the wicked world of drinking), so that they can pursue some alternate lifestyle, as in some cults. These cloisters are the most closed Community Ships, since they are not interested in controlling anything except the behavior of their members.

The Israeli kibbutzim were created to be reformers, to settle in the ancient land and help establish a new state with socialist ideals. But in the hostile environment before the creation of the state, they had to be cloisters as well, for their own protection. Once the state was established, however, they became converters too, seeking to attract new immigrants to the movement as well as to spin off new kibbutzim when the existing ones grew too large. It should be noted that the kibbutz movement never reached 10 percent of the Israeli population, despite its dominant influence in the early governments of the state. As the country developed economically, many of them felt forced to industrialize, which forced them to forgo their rather pure form of both socialism and communityship.

The Pros and Cons of the Community Ship

These are fascinating organizations, for better and for worse. They house some of the most exciting movements in organizations as well as some of the worst violations of human rights. Beliefs that are held so deeply can take an organization to some amazing heights of performance as well as to some shocking depths. (Witness some of the populist political movements of today and yesteryear.) **Community Ships can inspire us and they can enslave us, sometimes indistinguishably.** The logo at the outset of this chapter, which shows inward arrows that form a protective halo around the organization, also point to possible implosion.

Between Isolation and Assimilation

If the Divisional Form stands on the edge of a cliff, then **the Community Ship walks along a narrow ridge, advancing its mission between the danger of isolation on one side and that of assimilation on the other**.

The cloisters, especially, may be drawn increasingly toward isolation, to serve themselves. But no organization can be a pure closed system, because every one needs some inputs from the outside, at the very least, new people from time to time. Connecting out, however, raises the danger of assimilation—becoming contaminated by contact with the outer world. Too much of this and the organization may survive, but not as a Community Ship.

Between the *Wisdom of Crowds* and *Groupthink*

There are two popular, contradictory theories that can help explain the pros and cons of the Community Ship. In *The Wisdom of Crowds*, James Surowiecki wrote that "under the right circumstances, groups are remarkably intelligent, and are often smarter than the smartest

people in them."[114] In *Groupthink*, Irving Janis described the inclination of people in a tight-knit group to suffer the loss of creativity,
uniqueness, and independent thinking.[115] Look for both of these in
Community Ships.

Changing the Culture

Karl Weick wrote that "a corporation doesn't *have* a culture. A corporation *is* a culture. That's why they're so horribly difficult to change."[116]
And not only a corporation: imagine trying to change the culture of
any Community Ship that is intent on changing the world, but not its
own word.

Compelling cultures tend to mute any political activity that could
challenge them. People here are not supposed to build private alliances, not to hoard budgets or blow the whistle on their colleagues.
Of course, strategic candidates can be promoted, and lording is one
game commonly found in Community Ships, played by members who
flaunt their culture over others. Conflicts can also arise over the interpretation of the word, and become quite heated as each side pro-
fesses to be the more pure. But these conflicts must remain inside,
the members being quite careful about what outsiders see. Consider
those Talmudic scholars who fight furiously with each other over the
interpretation of the words in their ancient books, yet close ranks to
present a united front to the outside world.

CHAPTER 16

The Political Arena

Comedian Rodney Dangerfield used to quip: "I went to a fight the other night, and a hockey game broke out." Conflict can be found in every organization—agendas vary, personalities clash, influencers seek a better deal. Any of these can flare up to engulf the place in politics. The most programmed machine, the most secure entrepreneur, the most established culture can be challenged, whether arbitrarily for advantage or because some fundamental condition has changed.

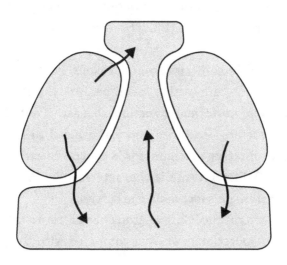

When conflict dominates, the organization can be described as a Political Arena, like a bunch of crabs clawing at each other in a bucket. **All the legitimate forms of authority get displaced, suspended, or exploited, as political games abound.** The conflicts can range from a focused confrontation to a free-for-all with skirmishes all over the place as various influencers pile in.

We are all aware of nation-states where chaotic politics took over, sometimes descending into civil war. In business, I heard about a family firm where two brothers—one in charge of production, the other sales—became so estranged that they ceased to speak with each other. You can imagine what happened in the rest of the place.

Conflict in an organization can develop gradually or flare up suddenly, often one followed by the other. Of course, simmering conflict is a lot more sustainable than outright hostility. (Witness the ongoing debates in your government's legislature.) No organization can sustain itself as a full-fledged Political Arena, unless it operates in some artificially privileged position that covers its losses, such as a government agency with secure funding or a company with a monopoly position in the marketplace. I once served on a committee that tried to mediate a long-standing battle in our university between left and right wingers in the economics department. I visited their offices to have a look. Prominent on the door of one protagonist was a newspaper article about the dispute. It had been there so long it had turned yellow!

This chapter will be short, for several reasons. First, there is no need to describe the structure of this form, because **the Political Arena has no structure**, no formal structure at least. (Politics does have its informal structure—in those political games.) In fact, **although one of the coordinating mechanisms is central to each of the other six forms, the Political Arena is characterized by the centrality of none.** Coordination gets lost amid the battles.

Second, the cons of the Political Arena need little attention because they are widely appreciated, at least compared with the pros, which will be the focus of the rest of the chapter. And third, the Political Arena is often temporary—a stage more than a state—and thus will receive additional attention in Chapter 19, for the role it plays in some of the transitions between the forms.

The Pros of the Political Arena

Perhaps no question dominates the literature of organizations more than "How can we change this place?" The one answer I don't think I have ever heard is "Make the place more political." **When the established forces of authority, expertise, and/or culture overwhelm an organization's capability for change, politics may have to be the way forward.** The organization has to be pulled apart before it can be put back together again. The Political Arena to the rescue!

We all know full well how divisive politics can be. Just as excessive culture can cause an organization to implode, so too can excessive conflict cause an organization to explode. What we must understand equally well, however, is that intense conflict can stop an organization from exploding as well as imploding. In Chapter 13, we considered the pros of politics in organizations. Here, we consider the pros of divisive politics that overwhelm an organization, two in particular.

First, **when an established order of power has outlived its usefulness, a Political Arena that flares up may be able to remove it.** In other words, intense conflict can sometimes be the only way to dislodge legitimate power that has become counterproductive—obsessive control, outmoded expertise, detached leadership, spent culture.

Hence, no matter how illegitimate its own power may be, the Political Arena can function as the functional bridge from one legitimate system of influence to another. Just as anarchists who lurk in every society may be able to foment revolution when large segments of the population have been repeatedly stymied, so too can politics, which lurks in every organization, be able to foment change that has been widely perceived as necessary but repeatedly stymied.

Second, **the Political Arena can speed up the inevitable demise of**

a spent organization. While many small organizations in deep trouble simply disappear (as in the bankruptcy of a company), large ones have influential stakeholders—shareholders, managers, unions—who can act to sustain them, for example, by lobbying for government support. From society's perspective, however, the sooner the demise comes, the better: political actors, like the scavengers that swarm over a carcass, can speed up the recycling of their useful resources.

I am no fan of organizational politics and have no wish to work in a Political Arena. (A taste of it once was more than enough.) But I do accept, and hope that I have persuaded you to accept, that this form of organization, like the others, has a constructive place in our societies. Organizational politics may irritate us, but it can sometimes serve us.

This completes the discussion of the seven forms alongside the seven forces. We turn now to how they play out.

PART VI

BALANCING THE FORCES ACROSS THE FORMS

It has been said that there are two kinds of people in the world: those who believe there are two kinds of people and those who don't. I'm not sure about that, but I do know that there are the *lumpers* of the world and there are the *splitters* (a distinction first made by Charles Darwin[117]). One synthesizes, the other analyzes. The lumpers create categories, according to the similarities in phenomena; the splitters zero in on the differences, and so like to take apart the lumps (and sometimes the lumpers too).

I am a consummate lumper, as you may have noticed—in this book, about seven lumps of organizing. The original version of the book brought out the splitters, who criticized its lumping. (One academic even referred to this, and related works by Danny Miller, as "McGillomania," in reference to our university.[118]) Practicing managers, however, have tended to be more sympathetic to the lumping—they have to get on with life instead of splitting theories.

Lumping, albeit imperfect, has certain benefits. It simplifies the complexities and appeals to our sense of order. Organizations can be quickly and easily understood—and, of course, misunderstood. When

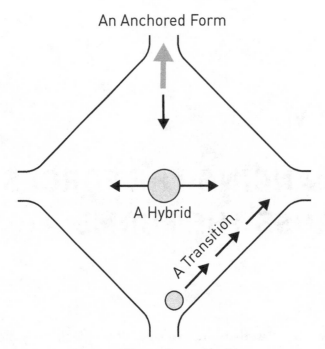

An Anchored Form

A Hybrid

A Transition

FIGURE VI.1 Forces Across the Forms

a form does fit, more or less, it can help to manage an organization—
for example, by suggesting possible causes for problems that arise. In
truth, we can't function without lumps. After all, words are lumps,
namely categories. (Consider *lumper*, *splitter*, and *McGillomania*.) We
would still be grunting at each other in caves without these word
lumps. Hence, **for clarification, for comprehension, for diagnosis,
and for prescription, we need lumping.**

And so, fit where necessary, but not necessarily fit. We can't ignore
the limitations of lumping, any more than the benefits of splitting.
There is always the nuancing of gray between the categorizing of black
and white. Hence, the perspective I wish to advance at this point in the
book is that our **lumping has to be modified by splitting. Put differently, we need to let the forces speak to the forms.** Along our way, in
fact, we have seen numerous anomalies in the forms, such as football
players who require extensive training in this most programmed of

sports and project organizations that need controllers to keep a lid on the volatility.

Of course, these are not anomalies, but reality—natural occurrences in organizations. They can be seen, in the diamond diagram repeated in Figure VI.1, in three aspects. Chapter 17 makes the case for *anchored forms* as preferable to pure forms. Chapter 18 introduces all sorts of *hybrids* of the forms, where two or more forces logically coexist in some kind of dynamic balance. And because organizations don't always hold still, Chapter 19 lays out a life cycle of *transitions* across the forms, when one prevalent force, or a combination of them, replaces another. It is especially these three chapters that map the space inside the diamond diagram, with the four forms at the nodes, to which the forces speak.

CHAPTER 17

In Praise of the Anchored Form

I have some bad news for you. Not only do none of the seven forms of organizations exist in the real world, but they should not exist. The forms don't exist because, as noted earlier, they are just words and diagrams on paper or screen—depictions of reality, not reality itself. And they should not exist because every organization is replete with nuances, complexities, and contradictions that cannot be ignored. But please don't put down this book quite yet. I will explain.

Figure 17.1 repeats the diamond diagram again, this time with all but one of the forces removed. With no countervailing force, the remaining one can propel the organization into outer space, so to

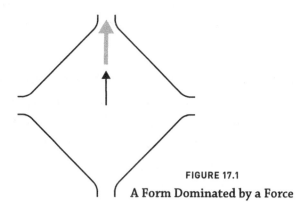

FIGURE 17.1
A Form Dominated by a Force

speak—out of control. A Programmed Machine can become so efficient that it drives everyone crazy, customers and workers alike, just as a Professional Assembly can become so proficient that it fails for want of efficiency. (In a hospital, soiled sheets can be as deadly as sloppy surgery.) In their purest versions, therefore, all the forms are flawed.

Here, then, we sing the praises of imperfection. **Because every form contains the seeds of its own destruction, an *anchored* version of the form, where some other force holds the dominant one in check, is better than the *pure* version.** Sure, many organizations come rather close to matching one of the forms, but to be effective, that had better not be too close. Hence, rather than throwing the forms out for lack of perfection, we just need to make sure that we understand their limitations.

We describe below a study that has illustrated how each of the four forms, dominated by one force, goes out of control. Then we discuss why this happens: because the dominating force *contaminates* the organization, hindering the use of other necessary forces. And this brings us to the blessings of *containment*—of the dominant force by one or more *countervailing* forces.

The Perils of Excellence

In his book *The Icarus Paradox*, author Danny Miller described four trajectories that take successful companies out of control—the perils of excellence, if you like.[119] They match our four forms rather well.

- **About the Personal Enterprise.** "The *venturing* trajectory converts growth-driven, entrepreneurial *Builders*, companies managed by imaginative leaders and creative planning and financial staffs, into impulsive, greedy *Imperialists*, who severely overtax their resources by expanding helter-skelter into businesses they know nothing about it."

- **About the Programmed Machine.** "The *decoupling* trajectory transforms *Salesmen*, organizations with unparalleled marketing skills, prominent brand names, and broad markets, into aimless, bureaucratic *Drifters*, whose sales fetish obscures design issues, and who produce a stale and disjointed line of 'me-too' offerings."

- **About the Professional Assembly.** "The *focusing* trajectory takes punctilious, quality-driven *Craftsmen*, organizations with masterful engineers and airtight operations, and turns them into rigidly controlled, detail-obsessed *Tinkerers*, firms whose insular technocratic cultures alienate customers with perfect but irrelevant offerings."

- **About the Project Pioneer.** "The *inventing* trajectory takes *Pioneers* with unexcelled R&D departments, flexible think-tank operations, and state-of-the-art products, and transforms them into utopian *Escapists*, run by cults of chaos-living scientists who squander resources in the pursuit of hopelessly grandiose and futuristic inventions."[120]

In another book, *The Neurotic Organization*, Miller and Manfred Kets de Vries suggest how each of our forms likely gets ill: the personal organization becomes *dramatic*, the machine organization becomes *compulsive*, the professional organization becomes *paranoid*, and the project organization becomes *schizoid* (plus the Divisional Form becomes *depressive*).[121]

The Dangers of Contamination and the Blessings of Containment

The advantages of a form are harmony and consistency as well as fit with its situation: each is a culture in its own right. The structure and processes are clear to the players, and so they can get on with their work.

But what if some necessary part doesn't quite fit—say, a research lab that has to create new products in a Programmed Machine? Then *contamination* can set in: the other parts try to make it conform. **Misfit is the debilitating weakness of the pure form: its dominant force tends to drive out other forces as somehow incorrect.** It's as tough to be a bureaucratic unit in an adhocracy as an adhocratic unit in a bureaucracy.

Okay, so to get around this, a Programmed Machine locates its research lab in the countryside, in the belief that the distance will shield it from the headquarters controls. Well, lead may block radiation, but what can block a determined technocrat? The controller drops in to have a look. It's 9:00 a.m. "Where is everybody? Can't these hotshots start at 8:30, like everybody else in this company?" (They left last night at 2:00 a.m., after struggling with some new software.)

Of course, the argument could be made that contamination is the price an organization has to pay for achieving consistency. After all, no organization can be all things to all people. Better to concentrate for clarity than to diffuse and confuse. Sure, but only with containment. **Because contamination by one force can sow the seeds of the destruction of a pure form, one or more other forces must contain that force—anchor it in place** (Figure 17.2).

While any of the other forces could do this, one may be most appropriate to contain each of the four forms. In both the Personal Enterprise and the Project Pioneer, efficiency may work best to contain an excess of personal power or unbridled creativity. Nothing like a few

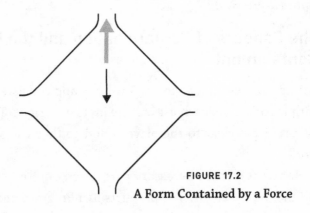

FIGURE 17.2
A Form Contained by a Force

technocrats to rein both in. In both the Programmed Machine and the Professional Assembly, as well as the Divisional Form and Community Ship, whose programs, protocols, targets, or beliefs can get too tight, collaboration for the sake of adaptation may have to serve as the countervailing force. Nothing like a creative team or two to open things up.

Culture and conflict can also serve as countervailing forces. In a hospital, a compelling culture can encourage physicians to collaborate, while in an entrepreneurial firm, a whistleblower might be able to limit the excesses of the chief. So, to make best use of the diamond framework, please see past the nodes in the corners, to the forces that lurk inside.

CHAPTER 18

Hail to the Hybrids

Many of the most interesting things, say the biologists, happen on the edges—on the interface between the woods and the fields, the land and the sea. There, living organisms encounter dynamic conditions that give rise to untold variety...but there is tension as well. The flora of the meadows, as they approach the woodlands, find themselves coping with increasingly unfavorable conditions: the sunlight they need might be lacking, and the soil no longer feels right.... The Edges, in short, might abound with life but each living form must fight for its own.[122]

—Ray Raphael, *Edges: Human Ecology of the Backcountry*

To function effectively, some organizations require that two or more forces coexist. The organization may oscillate between favoring one force or another, but ultimately it must maintain a *dynamic balance across them*. It must function, if you like, on the edges where these forces meet. **These are the *hybrids* of the world of organizations**, at least in terms of our framework.

For years, I sent out groups of students to study local organizations, after having exposed them to an early version of this book. When they were done, I gave them a list of questions (similar to the one in Chapter 11) to categorize their organization as one of the forms or some hybrid of them. Almost half the groups—57 out of 123—concluded that a hybrid best described their organization: they mentioned 17 kinds in all. Likewise, when I do workshops with managers and ask them which form or hybrid best fits their organization, while a number usually choose each of the forms, especially the Programmed Machine, the largest number, often around half, choose hybrids.

It may be helpful to limit the number of forms—not too many lumps in this cup of tea, thank you (7 will do)—but not so the number of hybrids. Any combination of two or more of the forms is conceivable. Our earlier discussion has already suggested several, including administrative adhocracies, snappy bureaucracies, personal conglomerates, and professional projects (Doctors Without Borders). However, **we can distinguish two main types of hybrids: blended ones, where two or more forms coexist across the whole organization, and assembled ones, where different parts of the organization use different forms**.

Blended Hybrids, of the Whole

Common in organizations are hybrids of personal leadership with some other prominent force. The symphony orchestra, for example, is, in fact, both top-down personal and bottom-up professional: the trained skills of its musicians blend with the personal 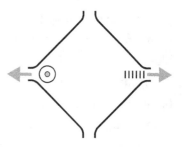 leadership of its conductor. At Apple with Steve Jobs at the helm, determined personal leadership blended with a great deal of project prospecting. Where safety concerns require high reliability—nuclear power plants, police forces—the trained skills of professionals have to blend with a profusion of machine-like rules.[123]

Assembled Hybrids, of the Parts

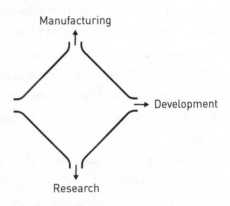

Examples of *differentiated* hybrids are also common: organizations that use different forms in their different parts. Many large banks, for example, have machine-like retail service for the mass market and more tailored project services for their investment banking. And how about the consulting firms that have one unit for executive search, more like a Professional Assembly, and another more like Project Pioneers for their consulting projects?

There are twenty-one possible combinations of the seven forms in pairs, and more still as threesomes and beyond. How about this? Once, after I did a presentation on the four forms, a manager from Apple came up to me and suggested that, while product designing was project, marketing and training tended to be more professional, and manufacturing more programmed. Add CEO Steve Jobs in that mix and Apple could have been described as a personal-project-professional-programmed hybrid! Likewise, pharmaceutical companies use project teams for research, professional skills in development, and machine-like programming in manufacturing (unless that is highly automated).

Cirque du Soleil is an extraordinary organization. Its events have been about as project pioneering as anyone can imagine. An EMBA student of ours, who had been in charge of training the acrobats, commented in a paper: "As a manager...you cannot let spreadsheets crush creative ideas...[you don't last long if you fail to] appreciate that fragility of creative thought." Yet these ideas are executed by highly trained, amazingly skilled performers, in Professional Assemblies, alongside the more programmed support staff that do all the mundane tasks associated with these events. And don't forget Guy

Laliberté—the nomad who joined the billionaire class with his reengineering of the circus. Personally, he provided the ideas for the shows.

Cooperation, Competition, and Cleavage

Hybrids don't experience the contamination found in the purer forms, because the different forces hold each other in check. Instead **hybrids experience *cleavage*, namely conflict along the fault lines, the edges where the different forces meet**.

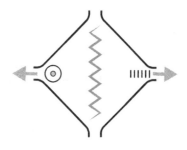

Fellini made a film called *Prova d'orchestra*, in which the musicians revolt to get rid of their conductor, only to discover that they could not function without him after all. The same can be said for other hybrids that wish to make beautiful music: **the diverging players have to cooperate despite their inclination to compete.** No pharmaceutical company wants to see its scientists in research battling with its professionals in development, any more than these developers battling with the marketers.

An important conclusion that comes out of this discussion, of contamination as well as cleavage, is that **the effectiveness of any organization depends on the management of *contradiction*.** The conflicts that arise from competing forces need to be faced, and alleviated, not ignored, ideally through mutual adjustment by the people directly involved.

CHAPTER 19

Riding the Life Cycle across the Forms

Many organizations spend much of their lives in one structure, where they get on with an established mission. For example, a symphony orchestra is likely to be a personal-professional hybrid no matter who is the conductor. But in the world of organizations, nothing is sacred. From time to time, most organizations have to, choose to, or are forced to, transition to some other structure, whether another form, or a hybrid. This chapter describes what seems to be a pattern of the common transitions, as a life cycle of organizations.

Here are some postulates about the main characteristics of these transitions.

- A transition can be rapid or gradual, complete or partial, permanent or temporary. Much as a supersaturated liquid freezes suddenly when it is disturbed, so too when its founder departs can a Personal Enterprise freeze rather quickly and permanently into a Programmed Machine. This suggests that **organizations, too, can experience *punctured equilibrium*: long periods of stability interrupted by occasional bursts of change.** But gradual transition is also possible, suspending an organization temporarily between the old and the new, or oscillating between them, as when a founder who stays at the helm of a growing mass production company gradually gives way to the formalized controls of the staff analysts.

- A transition can be (a) *expected naturally*, as when a new school makes an early transition from the personal toward the professional form, (b) *imposed* by particular influencers, as when a government forces the public schools to act more programmed than professional, or (c) caused by an *unexpected external disturbance*, as when a strike by the teachers of these schools forces them to consolidate power around a single superintendent.

- A transition can be smooth or conflictive, either way, functional or dysfunctional. When the founder quits a Personal Enterprise, the transition to a Programmed Machine can be rather smooth, whereas other transitions can be accompanied by considerable conflict, which can be functional when the transition is necessary, otherwise it is dysfunctional.

A Life Cycle Model of Organization Structure

We can delineate several stages—as leading tendencies, not imperatives—of a life cycle model of organization structure. These are summarized below and described in turn.

1. Organizations are usually born as Personal Enterprises, as in *start-ups*.

2. In youth, many sustain this form, at least partially, so long as their founder remains.

3. As they mature, organizations tend to settle into whatever structure fits most naturally with their conditions.

4. The settled life of a mature organization can be interrupted by impromptu transitions, whether championed by internal actors, imposed by external influencers, or driven by a change in circumstances.

5. Stagnating organizations—in mid life crisis, so to speak—can sometimes be renewed by transition to another structure, whether temporarily, as in the *turnaround* of a machine organization by a personal leader, or more permanently, as in the introduction of adhocratic elements to a bureaucratic structure.

6. Organizations can die of natural causes, as when they run out of funding, but some of the largest have to be brought down in the form of a Political Arena.

Birth: Start-Up as Personal Enterprise

Organizations are usually created as Personal Enterprises, for several reasons. First, most everything in a new organization has to be developed from scratch. Somebody has to find the resources, bring in the people, set up the facilities, and consolidate all of this around a new structure and culture, as well as a new strategy (unless defined at the outset). This gives founding chiefs considerable informal influence alongside their formal authority, which may last as long as they remain at the helm.

Second, direct supervision is the most natural coordinating mechanism at the outset of an organization, since people tend to turn to the chief for guidance. Mutual adjustment, in contrast, can be limited until the people get to know each other, and it takes time to establish standards.

Third, new organizations require, and tend to attract, chiefs with an entrepreneurial bent—enthusiastic builders, often rather visionary, even charismatic—to whom other people are drawn. Such founders like to grab the reins of something new, free of the constraints of the established organizations they know too well—to "do their own thing." This can be an exciting ride for all involved.

The term *entrepreneur* may be commonly associated with start-ups in business, but *social entrepreneurship* is prevalent in start-ups in the plural sector, and so is what can be called *public entrepreneurship* for start-ups in government. New NGOs, new community associations, new cooperatives, new government agencies all require the same strong initial leadership for the reasons just discussed.

Youth: Sustaining Partial Personal Enterprise

Personal leadership at the outset can sometimes sustain itself, at least partially, as long as the organization grows with its founder. After all, it was built around this person's own style, and perhaps vision as well. Plus the initial staff may remain loyal, even beholden, to the person who hired them and with whom they have likely developed a close, personal relationship. Moreover, as strong-willed individuals, founding leaders are often able to sustain a substantial degree of personal control. Think of all the famous businesses, unions, and other organizations that have grown remarkably large under personal leadership: the Amazons, Apples, and Teamsters.

Maturity: Settling into a Natural Structure

As they mature, most organizations end up with the structure most naturally suited to their conditions. We have seen numerous examples of this, ranging from hospitals as Professional Assemblies to orchestras as personal-professional hybrids.

Some organizations, of course, go nowhere else. The Personal Enterprise is their natural structure, continuing to suit them even as they develop. Big retail chains can thrive with a hands-on management that makes pressing decisions faster than would a "professional" management inclined to rely on analysis. A two-hundred-store retail chain might, after all, be managed as a one-store retail chain repeated two hundred times. Regular visits to a few of them can sometimes keep the CEO in touch with the whole of them.

Pivoting away from Personal Leadership

More commonly, however, personal leadership eventually becomes a liability. Grounded managing can become micromanaging, with the

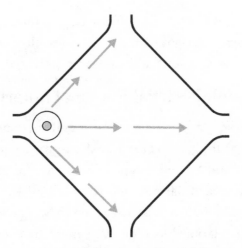

FIGURE 19.1 **Settling into a Natural Form**

chief overwhelmed by the details, or it can become macromanaging, as the chief tires of the details and decides to lead from on high. Think of the legacies destroyed by entrepreneurs who diversified their businesses in the belief that they could manage anything.

Hence, **as they mature, most organizations make a pivotal transition away from the personal organization**, if not to some hybrid (the intermediate arrows of Figure 19.1), then to any of the other forms (the following arrows), as discussed below.

To a Professional Assembly The pivotal transition from the personal organization toward the professional one can happen rather quickly. Consider a general hospital. From Day 1, alongside the founding chief arrive highly trained professionals, all ready to use their skills once the facilities and equipment are in place. Hence a natural transition can begin almost immediately—at least to an intermediate hybrid of the personal and professional forms so long as the founder remains.

To a Programmed Machine Probably the most common transition of all is from the Personal Enterprise to the Programmed Machine—especially in business, since so much of it is about mass production or mass service, founded by private entrepreneurship. As discussed earlier, this transition can be rather smooth: replace the founder with that professional management, and off you go. But if the founder refuses to leave, political games may be required to drive him or her out—whistle blowing to the board, perhaps, or the insurgency game. (Think of the mass movements that have been required to unseat so many autocratic rulers.)

To a Project Pioneer The project organization, like the professional one, tends to emerge quickly, especially when an organization begins with a project—for example, a firm of architects with a first commission. But the full transition can be prolonged when a strong chief is required to ensure collaboration in and across the teams.

To a Community Ship When a plural sector association begins with a compelling mission, the founding leader may have to yield power to more egalitarian communityship, which could be accompanied by conflict (famously in the case of Doctors Without Borders).

Midlife: Impromptu Transitions

The transitions so far described occur in the natural life cycles of organizations. But along the way can be impromptu transitions, championed by particular influencers or driven by unexpected changes. Several common ones are discussed below, some for the better, others for the worse.

Diversifying toward the Divisional Form

With a chief intent on accelerating growth, many successful businesses diversify and thus make a transition toward the Divisional Form. This transition is so common in businesses grown large that it may seem to be a natural one. (Some of the academic and popular literature has certainly made it seem so.) I put it here instead, as an impromptu transition, because "this ain't necessarily so."

For one thing, many successful businesses have "stuck to their knitting, more or less"—General Motors, for example.[124] For another, as discussed in Chapter 14, many of the corporations that have fully diversified, to become conglomerates, have eventually failed, or reconsolidated. Partial transition to an intermediate form of divisionalization seems to have worked better, for example, to the by-product or related product version in business (Panasonic), or the geographic version in plural sector associations (the Red Cross Federation).

Automating or Outsourcing Bureaucracy toward Adhocracy

As described earlier, by automating or outsourcing much of its operating work, a Programmed Machine can be left with an administrative structure that functions as a Project Pioneer: it concentrates on projects to design and maintain the automated facilities or negotiate the outsourcing contracts.

Settling Innovative Adhocracy into Professional Meritocracy

As they age, some operating adhocracies seek the calmer life of the Professional Assembly. Early in their careers, scientists, consultants, and other experts may be especially drawn to innovative work in teams—opportunities abound, the world is their oyster—and so they create or join Project Pioneers. But as they and their organizations age, these preferences can change. The excitement of project work can become unnerving, with its relentless boom-and-bust cycles. Those operating adhocracies that do project work for their clients can institutionalize their skills and settle down to become a Professional Assembly.

Then the battles can begin. "Enough change," say the meritocrats. "Let's concentrate on a few of our successes and tailor them to the needs of many clients." But the adhocrats want none of this. "What's done is done; let's find a new creative challenge."

When one group prevails, the organization either shifts to a

Professional Assembly or remains as a Project Pioneer. When neither does, it might divide in two, as do those management consulting firms discussed earlier: one part does ad hoc project work on contract while the other offers more standardized executive search services. Physicians in hospitals often split themselves personally in this way, doing their standardized clinical work alone and their more open-ended research in teams (although the former can contaminate the latter, driving much medical research, so-called, toward development, as the term is used in the pharmaceutical industry—for example, testing some existing medication on some new population).

Transition in the opposite direction—from the professional to the project form—while certainly possible (every conceivable transition is possible) is less likely. **The Professional Assembly, with its entrenched skills and dispersed power, is the most stable of all the forms and thus the most enduring.** Consider all the old universities still going strong after centuries, compared with the comings and goings of big corporations across decades.[125]

One other transition from the Project Pioneer is worth mentioning. When a project brings forth a new product of particularly high potential, there may be an inclination to give up the volatile life of the pioneer and exploit it, namely pivot to the stable life of a mass-production machine, and get rich.

Forcing Transition to Bureaucracy

As discussed, **external influencers and internal analysts often drive an inappropriate transition of any of the other forms toward the Programmed Machine**. Here is where that "one best way" thinking does its most damage.

As soon as any company goes public, no matter what its appropriate structure, stock market analysts can be at the door pushing for formalization. ("Can we please see your organization chart?") If a founder sells a Personal Enterprise to an established corporation, its analysts may descend on the place likewise. ("Do we have a Strategic Planning tool for you!") No wonder founders who stay on as CEO often leave soon after.

Of course, public sector departments and plural sector associations cannot issue shares or be sold. But many are dependent on funding agencies that have their own analysts, all ready with their technocratic controls. ("If you are not measuring it, how can you possibly be managing it?")

A small Personal Enterprise no more needs an organization chart than a Professional Assembly needs measures that drive its professionals to distraction. And why must they all go through the motions of some Strategic Planning ritual? To summarize, **a narrow form of technocratic managerialism runs rampant in our organizations and thus contaminates our societies.**

Aging: Renewal for Survival

Sooner or later, every organization has to expect the unexpected, no matter how stable its structure. The survival of a business can be threatened by a new competitor; a pandemic can throw a government into turmoil. As they age, healthy organizations revitalize: they find ways to renew themselves when necessary, although some forms do this more easily than others.

The Project Pioneer renews naturally, and constantly, within its existing form, thanks to the unique projects that come and go. As we saw with the rise of feature films in the National Film Board of Canada, one novel project can take the whole place to a new strategy.

The Professional Assembly can be highly adaptive at the operating level—think of the constant upgrading of medical protocols in hospitals. But with its power so diffused, and with the many standards imposed by the professional associations, the overall organization can be extremely resistant to renewal, no matter how necessary.

The Personal Enterprise, in contrast, can be as adaptive as its chief. One may be inclined to entertain all sorts of radical changes—except for the power system itself—while another may want to keep everything intact.

In the Community Ship, where everything tends to be sacred, renewal can be resisted fervently by adherents who would rather fight than switch. Here, then, can be found some of the most intense Political Arenas. But when isolation threatens its survival, the Community Ship may have to come ashore, so to speak—that is, moderate its culture and transition toward another structure.

The prize for resisting renewal, however, often has to go to the Programmed Machine, not only because everything is so tight, but also because the preferred way to fix any problem is to tighten it further: more planning, more measures, more rules, rules, rules. But rationalizing is not renewing. Hence, what is so often seen as the all-time one best way, from Taylor to today, can be the all-time worst way to renew an organization.

There has developed a massive literature on how to change organizations, most of which is actually about how to change the stagnating machine organization, often, in effect, by taking it toward another form. **_Job enlargement_ takes the machine organization toward the professional form, _innovative teamwork_ takes it toward the project form, and _turnaround_ takes any form to the personal organization, temporarily.** Each is discussed in turn.[126]

Enhancing Proficiency through Job Enlargement

By strengthening the proficiency of its workforce, a machine organization can transition toward a professional one, in three successive steps (Figure 19.2).

First, **job expansion** can increase the scope of positions in the operating core. For example, the jobs in a call center can be redesigned so that each addresses a wider variety of customer questions. Second, **people empowerment** can give the operating employees greater control over their own work—for example, to decide together who goes on which shift. And third, **skill enhancement** can upgrade the

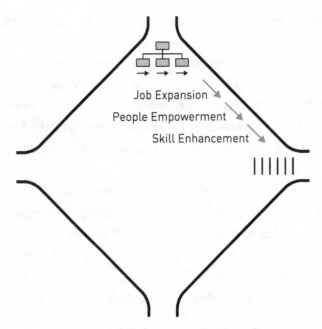

FIGURE 19.2 **Job Enlargement in Three Steps**

capabilities of the operating employees, so that they get closer to professional status, and the structure closer to the professional organization. These call center operators, beyond giving pat answers, can be trained to work out the customers' problems with them. The COVID pandemic, by the way, enlarged many jobs because people working at home were less directly supervised by their managers.

Encouraging Innovation through Teamwork

Any structure in need of more innovation can likewise take three successive steps toward more of a project structure.[127] Figure 19.3 shows this with regard to the machine organization, where such efforts are most likely to be attempted.

Initially, the organization can add a **separate unit** to carry out innovative projects on behalf of the whole organization, as when a manufacturing company sets up a research lab to develop new products. But if contamination of this unit sets in, the organization can take

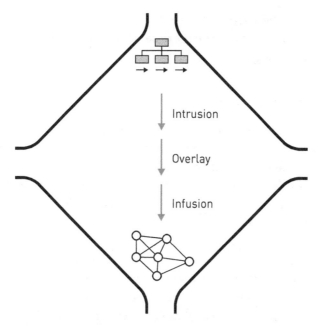

FIGURE 19.3 **Collaborative Innovation in Three Steps**

a further step by laying **adhocratic teams** over its formal structure, drawing their members from various units.[128] Creative people from engineering, manufacturing, and marketing, perhaps with an outside customer, can work together across traditional boundaries to develop new products.

Finally, when a truly significant shift to widespread innovating is necessary, the organization can try to **infuse a culture of innovation** throughout its structure. This way, everyone can contribute ideas, as in the use of *kaizen* (continuous improvement) in Japanese companies. Toyota "views employees not just as pairs of hands but as knowledge workers . . . [with] the wisdom of experience . . . on the company's front lines."[129] In a highly Programmed Machine, however, this last step is more easily said than done, which explains why, when a new technology radically alters a product, the established manufacturers are usually outsmarted by new entrants in the industry—likely to be Project Pioneers. They don't need the intrusion of innovation because they have a profusion of it already. But not so the Professional Assemblies, whose structures can be more set than those of the Programmed Machines (see box).

COLLABORATION ... FINALLY

During a months-long study of a large teaching hospital in Montreal, I attended nineteen committee meetings—of the Medical Executive Committee, Nursing Executive Committee, Management Committee, and the Board (a committee for each silo). A crisis of overloading in the Emergency Room, festering for years; was discussed in almost all these meetings, to no avail.

This was not a medical problem, nor a nursing problem, nor a management problem, nor a board problem. It was a hospital problem. Yet the one committee that had representation from all of these silos had not met for months! Finally the government threatened a major cut in the hospital's budget if the ER problem was not resolved. An ad hoc committee was created of doctors, nurses, and managers, chaired by the assistant head of nursing. Soon it resolved the problem. A simple project overlaid on a Professional Assembly can go a long way.[130]

Turning around through Personal Leadership

Any other organization in need of significant renewal most commonly reverts temporarily to the Personal Enterprise, to enable a new chief to effect a *turnaround*. Again, this is shown in Figure 19.4 in three steps, from the Programmed Machine, where we can expect it to be most common.

This happens for the same reason that organizations rely on personal leadership at their birth: direct supervision can be the fastest and most integrative mechanism for coordination. Bring in the new chief, suspend the established rules to allow him or her to make the necessary changes, and, once done, if appropriate, take the organization straight back to where it was, for example, to consolidate as

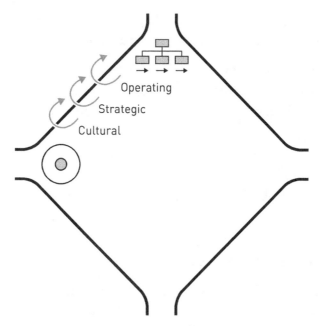

FIGURE 19.4 **Turnaround in Three Steps**

a renewed machine—and sometimes rid itself of the savior who no longer fits.[131]

Three kinds of turnaround can be described—operating, strategic, and cultural—in steps toward deeper changes.

1. **Operating turnaround.** This concentrates the renewal in the operations, to render them more functional. One lauded CEO turned around a British manufacturer of trucks by focusing his personal attention on the treatment of the workers in the factory, which resulted in a marked improvement in productivity. Operating turnaround is the easiest of the three because it keeps the strategies and systems largely intact. But it can also be the weakest, because the changes can be cosmetic—a veneer that washes off in the first crisis.

2. **Strategic turnaround.** This repositions the organization in its environment, or brings in a whole new strategic perspective. A

manufacturing company may add product lines, a government department may charge for a service that was previously free.

3. **Cultural turnaround**. This takes renewal farthest, to renew a culture that has atrophied. Since organizations don't have cultures, but are cultures (as Karl Weick was quoted earlier), restoring what's left of a good culture may be easier than trying to create a new one in its place. In one declining company that I came across, remnants of the culture that had made it successful remained, at least in the hearts of some of the old-timers, in the vestigial places from which it could grow back, much as an octopus can regenerate a lost limb.

Renewal in the Other Forms

Turnaround need not be restricted to the machine form. A Personal Enterprise itself can be turned around with a new chief, since power is already concentrated in one place. Not infrequently, retired founders have come back to revive their own enterprises that were faltering under their successors.

In the Professional Assembly the professionals are inclined to defer to no one, least of all a chief who suddenly wants to call the shots. Hence, overlaying a project team on the professional structure may be preferred when possible (as described above in the box on the hospital ER team). But when a crisis is severe enough, the political games that arise may have to be suspended to give a new chief time to fix the place for everyone's benefit.

The situation of turnaround in the Project Pioneer can be similar, except that this form of organization is so used to changing that it can often self-renew before someone is needed to turn it around.

The Role of Politics in Renewal

Finally, failing all of the above, **when an organization lacks the necessary capacity for self-renewal, political games may have to force it to change**—for example, by challenging the existing culture, defying the outmoded rules, sabotaging the intrusive measures. Look for insurgency games, whistle-blowing, rival camps, and more. If this doesn't work, because the organization is too far gone, it may have to face the final stage in its own life cycle, just as we do in our own lives.

Demise: Natural or Political

Can a failed organization rise from its own ashes, the way the mythical phoenix does every five hundred years? Should it? The business press revels in reporting such stories of resurrection, compared with reporting the far more common stories of over-and-out demise, sometimes after fixes that have failed repeatedly. **Fixing a failing organization can be as mythical as that phoenix.**

Organizations age and atrophy, just as humans do. As time goes by, joints stiffen, channels block, parts degenerate. Turning inward if they can, for protection as closed systems, may serve certain stake-holders temporarily, but not the society around them.

Organizations on Life Support

Do we need so many ailing organizations sustained by their established wealth or political influence? We are inundated with geriatric consulting—that's where the money is—compared with pediatric, even obstetric, consulting. Enormous effort goes into trying to make sclerotic machine organizations "agile," or "getting elephants to dance."

But do we need machines to be agile, or have to put up with elephants forced to dance? As discussed, machines are generally made for specialized purposes. When they cease to be necessary, or efficient, we don't adapt them, we get rid of them, and recycle their parts. So too with our Programmed Machines, if not our Project Pioneers, which are meant to be agile.

If this sounds brutal, please understand that I am responding in kind: the ailing organizations are rarely the compassionate ones, compared with younger, more energetic ones that can be built on their ashes. Did not the economist Joseph Schumpeter rightfully sing the praises of "creative destruction" in our economies?[132] Besides, since most of these spent organizations are likely to die soon anyway, why prolong the agony, and the expense? Wouldn't it be more productive if they died of a quick stroke, instead of suffering through a prolonged illness?

A healthy society maintains a steady flow of fresh, new organizations to replace its exhausted old ones. In other words, **it is not the renewal of single organizations that should concern us so much as the renewal of our society of organizations**. Smaller organizations usually die quickly, largely unnoticed, thus enabling their resources to be recycled immediately. The problem lies with the large ones that have the power to sustain themselves politically, with the support of their owners and executives (who willingly suspend their praise of "free enterprise"). This is often supported by elected governments, of all stripes, that are inclined to rescue big bankrupt businesses for fear of suddenly losing one mass of employment, while far more employment is steadily lost with the smaller bankruptcies.

Demise as a Political Arena

Eventually some of these big organizations are brought down by the very political activities that may have sustained them in their dying days. They become Political Arenas, overrun with political games, as all sorts of influencers scavenge what remains of them. Another great legacy succumbs, while the messy world of organizations does, finally, carry on.

Now let's get back to life, agile life.

PART VII

ORGANIZING BEYOND SEVENS

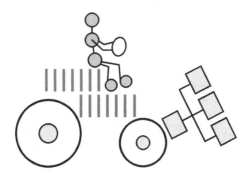

Every once in a while, a question comes along that stops us in our tracks. Alain Nöel, when he was a doctoral student at McGill before joining École des hautes études commerciales de Montréal, asked me such a question. Having read an early draft of the original version of this book, Alain asked: **Was I playing jigsaw puzzle or LEGO with these pieces?** In other words, were they meant to be assembled into a few established forms, or to be used to create new ones (as LEGO was, before it added so many three-dimensional jigsaw puzzles to its product lines).

I realized that I had been playing jigsaw puzzle but should start playing LEGO. All those "anomalies" that didn't fit a form, or even a hybrid of them, could become opportunities to see beyond the forms. Hence I created a file called "LEGO," into which I put the misfits. The final part of this book celebrates this misfitting. Why stop at seven?

From Pat to Playful My dictionary defines a puzzle as something difficult to understand. Therefore a jigsaw puzzle is not a puzzle, since it is easy to understand, no matter how difficult it may be to assemble. In a jigsaw puzzle:

1. The pieces are supplied.
2. Each is clean cut.
3. They fit together perfectly...
4. to make the picture on the box.

This is pat, not puzzling. In contrast, here are the characteristics of a true puzzle:

1. The pieces have to be found, or created.
2. Each appears as an obscure fragment.
3. Seldom do these pieces fit together neatly; somehow they have to be connected.
4. With no box in sight, the picture has to be concocted from these fragments and connections.

To solve such puzzles, **we have to be playful, not pat: open ourselves to the creative construction of novel structures**—for our organizations and otherwise. Hence this final part of the book is titled "Organizing Beyond Sevens." Chapter 20 describes how organizations open up their boundaries, and Chapter 21 discusses how they can open up the *process* of designing their structures.

CHAPTER 20

Organizations Outward Bound

The term *outward bound* was originally used to describe ships departing their home port for foreign destinations. Later it came to be associated with an NGO that provides youth with adventures in nature. Here it can be used to describe what many organizations have been doing in recent years.

Bound has two quite opposite meanings. Besides that of going somewhere else—opening up—is that of closing in, "being restricted to or by a place or situation" (Oxford English Dictionary). This chapter discusses how **organizations that used to be bound by their borders have in recent times gone outward bound.**

Let's go back to that seven-year-old's question at the outset, about what is an organization, for example, an Apple. If you answer that it is the people who work for "Apple," what if she asks about the guy sweeping the floors in one of their stores: "Is he an apple too?" "No, he's on contract." "Huh?" If she looks at your phone and asks: "If this is an apple, why aren't those little things called apples instead of apps?" "Because Apple is a platform." "Like the stage at a concert?"

The boundaries of many organizations have indeed become blurred in recent times, with contracts for cleaning going out and apps for

connecting coming in. Many researchers and journalists have followed suit, by describing all this in ways that themselves are blurred.
This chapter seeks to bring some clarity to this. I noted in Chapter 1
that the first version of this book was subtitled "A Synthesis of the
Research," whereas this version is meant to be a synthesis of my experiences. Except in this chapter, which offers a synthesis of what looks
to be the most significant development in organization structuring in
recent times.[133]

We begin by describing how inwardly bounded organizational
structures used to be: sharp borders were maintained, even while
pursuing strategies called *diversification*. Then, along came a variety of
arrangements that have taken organizations outward bound. We discuss six: *networking out, contracting to outsource, partnering to venture
jointly, establishing a platform for others, affiliating for common purpose*,
and *associating around a table*.

If in the late twentieth century, the Project Pioneer became the
favored structure—in fact, by breaking down the boundaries *within*
organizations—then **these arrangements that break down the
boundaries *across* organizations have been having their full flowering in the twenty-first century.** All sorts of walls have come tum-
bling down.

Bounded by Diversification and Vertical Integration

For much of the twentieth century, the most prominent strategies of
large corporations were vertical integration and diversification, pursued within their traditional boundaries.

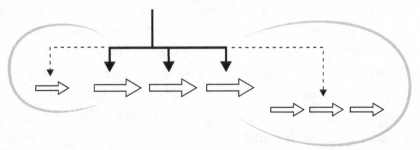

Vertical integration extended the chain of operations of the organization, to encompass suppliers at one end (*upstream*) and customers at the other (*downstream*), by bringing them inside its own boundaries. An automobile company might buy a supplier of its batteries, or create its own dealerships. Henry Ford pursued this strategy to an extreme: "To complete the vertical integration of his empire, he purchased a railroad, acquired control of 16 coal mines and about 700,000…acres of timberland, built a sawmill, acquired a fleet of Great Lakes freighters to bring ore from his Lake Superior mines, and even bought a glassworks."[134]

When it diversified, a company bought others in different businesses, and likewise brought them inside, or else developed new businesses internally, as did Honda, by exploiting its expertise in motors to produce a variety of other vehicles—outboard motors, lawnmowers, ATVs, and so on. Either way, the boundaries of these organizations usually remained sharply delineated, with the new activities reporting through its established hierarchy of authority. Under Henry Ford you were Ford. Period.

How this has changed!

Networking Outward

Networking is hardly new. In our institutional lives, like our personal ones, we have always networked to facilitate communication, externally as well as internally. **What has changed in re-** 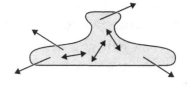 **cent times, thanks to the new social media, is the reach of networking externally.** Connecting with associates around the world can sometimes be easier than connecting with neighbors next door. At the end of their shift in Boston, a team of software engineers can transfer the work where they left off (*asynchronously*) to a team in Bangalore, which will continue the work until they transfer it back at the end of their shift, all with remarkable seamlessness.[135]

Networking need not be based on any formal structural arrangement; it can just happen, for the sake of coordination by mutual adjustment. In contrast, the other five arrangements of outward bound are somewhat formally structured—two by making use of contracts, another of rules, the last two of designated membership.

Contracting to Outsource

An organization's boundaries begin to blur when it engages in *outsourcing*—the opposite of vertically integrating—as some activities pre-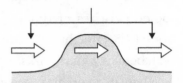**viously done in-house are contracted to outside organizations or individuals.** For example, most companies these days contract out the cleaning of their offices, and many engage executive search firms to help them find new managers. In these cases, the supplier is not *in* the organization, but not quite *out* of it either, because it supplies its services on a regular basis, under contract, for a negotiated period of time.

How about this for an example? Once, when visiting a factory, I was told that the workers in blue were employees of the company whereas those in green were not: they were doing similar work, but received their paychecks from another company. Talk about blurring the boundaries: this one was evident only in the color of the work clothes!

Some outsourcing has been around for a long time.[136] Most every organization has always bought on contract, for example, legal services. And *contractors* in the construction industry have long used an extensive form of outsourcing. As their name suggests, they secure the contract to construct a building and then *subcontract* the activities—electrical, plumbing, scaffolding, and so forth—to a host of specialized companies. Not so different is a film company that decides what film to make and then engages independent directors, scriptwriters, actors, editors, and so on to make it.

If the recent wave of outsourcing has come partly in reaction to the excesses of vertical integration (Henry Ford–style), now the pendulum can have a tendency to swing the other way. It's one thing for a retailer to contract out the maintenance of its stores, quite another to let go of, say, the sourcing of its merchandise (Amazon?). And while extensive contracting may work in the film business, it risks hollowing out the essence of some other organizations. Key here is to figure out what are the organization's *core competencies*—those it cannot let go without being a viable operation, such as securing the contracts and choosing the subcontractors in those construction companies.[137] Sometimes, however, an organization can be surprised by what turns out to be a core competence. Was this the case with Air Canada that developed a highly successful points program called Aeroplan, then spun it into a separate division, later sold it, and finally bought it back?

Outsourcing has, of course, hardly been restricted to business. In the plural sector, years ago my own university converted many of its administrative staff to contracts, which in my opinion has weakened its culture. And outsourcing has long been prominent in government, if not by that name. With so many services to provide, it has long used outside suppliers for much that could have been done inside. In fact, many NGOs exist to provide public services on contract—say, programs to feed the poor. More recently, the *New Public Management* (discussed in Chapter 14) may have been driving the outsourcing of public services to excess, perhaps like those American states that have outsourced prison services to private companies.

It is worth noting that outsourcing, and some of the other arrangements to be discussed, have been taking organizations toward the project structure, for the same reason as have the automating of their operations. With the shedding of some internal activities, more of their administrative work functioned as projects—for example, to negotiate external contracts instead of having to manage internal functions.

Partnering to Venture Jointly

Here the borders blur further, as independent organizations partner to design, develop, and/or market particular products or services. They venture 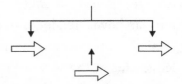 **jointly, and temporarily.** For example, "an idea travels from innovation to commercialization through at least two different companies, with the different parties involved dividing the work of innovation."[138]

The Smart Car was an interesting example of this in the automotive industry, resulting from a joint venture of Mercedes and Swatch, of all things. And the vaccine breakthrough in the COVID pandemic came from a joint venture of Pfizer with the husband and wife team of a small company.[139] Watch a feature film today and you will likely see a whole list of "producers."

Here again, the arrangement is hardly restricted to business. The label *joint venture* may be favored by business, but that of PPP (public-private partnership) is commonly used for joint ventures across two of the sectors. In fact, many that go by this label are really public-plural partnerships, while public-plural-private partnerships (not yet called PPPPs) are not uncommon, as when local governments, companies, and NGOs partner to reduce pollution in their city.

Offering a Platform for Others

The other face of outsourcing is what might be described as insourcing: **an organization sets itself up as a** *platform* 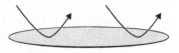 **for the particular use of outsiders.** Coordination on the platform, between supplier and user, even between users who meet there, as on eBay, tends to be largely by mutual adjustment, but electronically.

Wikipedia is an archetypical example of the platform organization, as is open-source software. To use the words of Wikipedia about OSS: "the copyright holder grants users the right to use, study, change, and distribute the software and a source code to anyone and for any purpose."

I am not an employee of Wikipedia, not even a member. (It has no members. On its website: "How do you become a member of Wikipedia? Just go for it!") I am thus not inside Wikipedia, yet am I outside of it? I can go inside any time I like. How about now?

As I wrote this, I went in to Wikipedia and looked up "platform organization." Here is what I got: *"The page 'Platform organization' does not exist. You can ask for it to be created."* By myself, no less, so long as I follow some rules. (Facebook, another platform organization, found out what can happen when the rules are inadequate.) Imagine if I could do this with my supermarket: "I couldn't find tiger shrimp in your seafood list, so I added it. I will come by tomorrow to pick some up."

Wikipedia is a plural-sector organization with no owner—it's neither private property nor public property, but *common property*, available to all, like the ocean. (It funds itself by soliciting donations from its users.) Facebook, in contrast, is the private property of its shareholders, as are many other platform organizations. Yet its influence on our social discourse has caused it to be treated like common property, almost public property. More blurring of the traditional boundaries.

How to define the presence or absence of the boundaries of an organization like Wikipedia? As outlined in what Seidel and Stewart call the "new community architecture," or C-form, these plural-sector platforms have "(1) fluid, informal peripheral boundaries of membership; (2) significant incorporation of voluntary labor; (3) information-based product output; and (4) significantly open sharing of knowledge."[140]

On the more conventionally commercial side, some years ago American Airlines joint ventured with IBM to create SABRE, a platform that enabled "tens of thousands of travel agents and others . . . [to be] perfectly coordinated in . . . reservations for the flights, hotels and car rentals that are listed there." And, of course, Apple created the iPhone as a platform on which all kinds of organizations can offer their apps.[141]

Just as the gentleman in Molière's famous play discovered that he was speaking prose, so too are we discovering that we have been using such platforms for a long time—for example, food markets where farmers rent space to find their customers and stock markets where investors go to buy and sell their stocks.[142] And think about all the doctors who have long viewed hospitals as platforms where they practice their profession. Some companies have, in fact, sought to reframe their business as a platform for their own benefit. Uber, for example, prefers to be seen as a platform for drivers to sign up and find people to shuttle around. Funny, because I thought it was a taxi service that found an outsourcing way to keep its drivers at arm's length.

Affiliating for Common Purpose

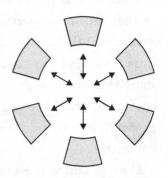

Affiliating is a kind of inserving (in contrast to outsourcing), where a group of organizations join together to provide themselves with one or more common functions. Thus do hospitals sometimes affiliate to negotiate with suppliers for better prices. (Together, these Professional Assemblies form an assembly.) Likewise, businesses create their Chambers of Commerce, sometimes to promote local tourism. (Ahrne and Brunsson have labeled these meta-organizations.[143])

Affiliating is similar to platforming, except that here the users create the platform for themselves, as members, with no single one in charge. In other words, they affiliate, but don't integrate, since each member maintains full independence. At the center of the assembly may be a small staff to hold it together, typically headed by someone in a member organization elected to a limited term of office. Compare the example used earlier of the small national accounting firms that affiliate to provide foreign services to each other with the global accounting firms, incorporated as single organizations, and so structured closer to the Divisional Form. Hence, the figure above depicts affiliation in the form of a donut, with the substance in the ring, not at the center.

Associating around a Table

What we are calling *associating* may appear to be similar to affiliating, but the distinction is worth making. It is looser than contracting, venturing, platforming, and affiliating, but still an arrange- 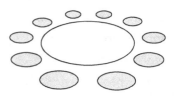 ment of organizations outward bound. Here, **organizations combine for convenience, with an established membership, to associate for common *concerns* rather than affiliate for specific *functions*.** The figure above depicts the associates, symbolically but often literally, sitting at a round table, where they meet periodically to discuss interests they share in common. Look for much of this in diplomacy—for example, in the G20 and G7, compared with NATO, which is an affiliation with a military function.

Popular terms such as *consortium*, *chamber*, *alliance*, and *assembly* may describe these associations, although some, as we have seen, are used for affiliations as well. Do the trade associations in industries discuss common concerns, or lobby for common causes? Often both. How about a few big competitors that get together periodically "just to chat, mind you"—whereas this association turns out to be a front for the affiliates of a cartel?

The Forms Outward Bound

All six arrangements can be found in any of the forms and hybrids, although more in some, less in others.

Perhaps less in the Programmed Machines, Personal Enterprises, and Community Ships: being predisposed to maintaining control, they can be disinclined to open their boundaries beyond some out-sourcing and associating. Perhaps more in the Project Pioneers that are naturally open and flexible, not only to take themselves outward bound with all these arrangements, but also to welcome other organizations inward bound—for example, by including outside employees on their own teams.

Likewise we should expect to find a good deal of all these arrangements in the Professional Assemblies. Their borders tend to be wide open, with many of their professionals inclined to network and joint venture, affiliate, and associate right and left, locally and globally. Notice how often media interviews of university professors happen when they are travelling abroad. Universities themselves also reach out in all kinds of ways—for instance, when they venture to create joint degree programs (see box).

MANAGEMENT EDUCATION OUTWARD BOUND

In Chapter 3, management was described as a practice that uses some art and much craft but limited science. The art of managing is innate—it cannot be taught—while the craft is not taught but learned, mostly through experience on the job. The science can be taught, in the form of analysis, but that is hardly management. Must we, therefore, leave the development of managers to informal mentoring and coaching on the job? Not necessarily: we can take the educational process outward bound.

Regular MBA programs tend to be self-contained, their borders quite firm: these programs are usually offered within a single school, taught by its own faculty. Most of this occurs in large classrooms where the students sit in tiered rows facing the *instructor*, who lectures or leads case study discussions about companies the students have not known. The curriculum is designed as an assemblage of separate courses in the business functions (marketing, finance, etc.), for students with little or no managerial experience. Hence the focus is on analysis, rather than the craft of managing.

Colleagues and I created the International Masters Program for Practicing Managers (impm.org) in 1996, to take management education to another place: namely management development. As social learning beyond traditional teaching, it opens the boundaries of management education to the experience of the participants, who are practicing managers. They learn in an open setting of small groups at round tables, where they spend half the time reflecting with each other on their personal experience, in light of the materials introduced by the faculty in the other half.

Five schools partner in the IMPM, each responsible for one *managerial mind-set* of ten days: the reflective mind-set (managing self) in Lancaster, England; the analytic mind-set (managing organizations) in Montreal, Canada; the worldly mind-set (managing context) in Bangalore, India; the collaborative mind-set (managing relationships) in Yokohama, Japan; and the action mind-set (managing action) in Rio de Janeiro, Brazil.

There are no courses in the IMPM, more like sessions, of a wide variety, that run typically from an hour to a day. Hence the program looks more like a Project Pioneer than a Professional Assembly. For example, *friendly consulting* provides each manager with opportunities to receive the advice of a team of colleagues on an issue of concern. All this is supplemented by other activities that take place in the manager's own workplace—for example, *managerial exchanges* whereby the managers pair up to spend the better part of a week observing and commenting at each other's workplace, and *impact teams* that the managers create to help carry their learning into their organizations.

In all of these ways, the IMPM takes management development outward bound, using the arrangements discussed in this chapter:

- The five schools form a joint venture. (One school does not outsource part of its own program to others.) They can also be seen to affiliate—for the common purpose of furthering management education.
- Much of the instructors' teaching is outsourced to the managers' learning: as *participants*, beyond students, they set the agendas for their discussions at the round tables, friendly consulting sessions, and impact teams at work.
- All this together has rendered the IMPM a platform on which innovation for management education has flourished. Aside from that discussed above, consider this use of the seating arrangements. Sometimes, one manager at each table is designated the *keynote listener*, to sit with his or her back to the others and listen to them.

In the debrief that follows, these keynote listeners form an inner circle to chat about what they heard, around which everyone else sits. Eventually, anyone else who wishes to add to the chat can tap the shoulder of someone in the inner circle, to replace him or her while the conversation continues.

- As a pedagogical platform, the IMPM welcomes guests, to take what they see back to their own institutions. McGill, with École des hautes études commerciales in Montreal, has also developed a similar EMBA program (call it Educating Managers Beyond Administration), while McGill alone has developed an International Masters for Health Leadership (mcgill.ca/imhl). CoachingOurselves.com has also been created as an enterprise (of which I am a partner) to use this form of social learning in the managers' own workplace. Small groups download conceptual materials and consider its use to improve their own organization. Here, management development opens its borders to organization development.[144]

I hope that this discussion will encourage you to go outward bound, in your own life as well as in and across your organizations, to address the puzzling puzzles that have been plaguing us for centuries. In the final chapter, we consider how to help make this happen.

CHAPTER 21

Opening Up Organization Design

We close this book by opening up the process of designing organizations. Here are some thoughts to keep in mind.

Customizing Design

Every one of us is unique. Hence every organization is unique, since it is made up of our unique selves. And so, every structure has to be customized, more or less, even if only to adapt to the idiosyncrasies of its people. Part II of this book introduced the building blocks of organization design, and Part III showed how these can be assembled into four different forms of organizations, like a jigsaw puzzle. Parts IV and V added more pieces to the puzzle—seven forces and three more forms—and Part VI used these forces to open the space between the forms, by showing how they moderate, combine, and transform themselves. Here, we consider how to **play LEGO: to construct structures that combine the pieces in customized ways.**

The eminent organization theorist Herbert Simon, in a book called *The Sciences of the Artificial*, wrote that "everyone designs who devises courses of action aimed at changing existing situations into preferred ones."[145] This include, not only architects who design buildings and engineers who design products, but also educators who design courses and managers who design structures, even authors who design books. How do they do this? Maybe not in the way you might think.

Four Approaches to Design

Jeanne Liedtka and I published an article titled "Time for Design," in which we identified four approaches to designing organizations.[146]

- A *formulaic* approach based on following preexisting principles more than engaging in open-ended experimentation.

- A *visionary* approach that relies on the personal imagination of the designer, thus affording more responsiveness to opportunity.

- A *conversational* approach that opens the process beyond the designer, to the insights of the people who have to live with the design.

- An *evolving* approach that enables the design process to keep adapting as situations change, problems arise, and opportunities appear.

The formulaic approach is pat rather than playful. By itself, it is insufficient for customized design. The other three approaches can be playful, by their use of imagination, conversation, and adaptation, respectively, to consider forces and forms, culture and conflict, efficiency and proficiency, centralization and decentralization, craft and creativity. We have learned quite a bit in this book from the bees, but please see an important exception in the box.

FLIES MAY BE BETTER DESIGNERS THAN BEES

"If you place in a bottle half a dozen bees and the same number of flies, and lay the bottle horizontally, with its base [the closed end] to the window, you will find that the bees will persist, till they die of exhaustion or hunger, in their endeavor to discover an [opening] through the glass; while the flies, in less than two minutes, will all have sallied forth through the open neck on the opposite side....

"It is [the bees']...very intelligence, that is their undoing.... They evidently imagine that the issue from every prison must be where the light shines clearest; and they act in accordance, and persist in too-logical action.

"To [bees] glass is a supernatural mystery...and, the greater their intelligence, the more inadmissible, more incomprehensible, will the strange obstacle appear. Whereas the feather-brained flies, careless of logic...flutter wildly hither and thither and meeting the good fortune that often waits on the simple...necessarily end up by discovering the friendly opening that restores their liberty to them."[147]

The moral of the story is that **we need more flies designing structures and fewer bees.**

Paving the Pathways

Think of designing this way. There is a park in Prague, also perhaps where you live, that was designed formulaically—by designers who knew better. They paved pathways where they decided that people should walk. One of these, designed to take people from a busy street to a bridge, was paved in an S-shape. The designers formulated, but the people of Prague did not implement. They took control of the situation and walked straight across, on grass that became earth. Thus evolved the people's pathway to the bridge.

This suggests that **there are two kinds of designers: those who really do know better, and those who, by believing they know better, do worse.** When a surgeon is about to begin an operation, we don't say: "Could you cut a little lower please?" The surgeon knows better. But an architect, educator, or manager who knows better can be a menace to good design, because this precludes the experience of the users.

There are, of course, architects who know what they don't know, and so allow the people to walk the park, so to speak. Their practice is visionary because it is open to the vision of the users. And it is conversational because it listens to the users, and this makes it evolving, because, as the walkers keep walking, the pathways keep changing.

None of this should be different in designing organizations. **Instead of designers who know better as they pave the structures for everyone else, the users who have to live the consequences of the structure need to participate in the design of it. They have to formulate by implementing: learn their way to the pathways that suit them best.**

Sally and Sam decide to start a project, and ask Sylvie to present it to management—that is, to be the de facto manager. As their efforts succeed, and consolidate, it may be time to pave their pathway (namely formalize their structure). But not too solidly, because no one can be sure when the pavement will have to be torn up for a better way.

Emergent Structure

Hence, **we must beware of immaculate conception in designing our organizations. Doing so in one shot, however common, leaves little room for the users to adapt and correct mistakes.** That's what the architect of the city of Brasilia did, to the chagrin of some of its residents to the present day. In a similar respect, I once spent a couple of days at a meeting in a house designed by Frank Lloyd Wright. I was told that the woman of the house hated the place: everything was fixed, even the furniture. That house remains famous: architects who have never lived there love it!

"An old saying has it that architecture is frozen music. With organizations, however, there is never even a momentary freeze" (this from Yoshinori Yokoyama, in a fascinating article titled "An Architect Looks at Organization Design").[148] **Organizations require emergent structures, just as they require emergent strategies: when possible, start marginally, tentatively, and let experience take it from there.** In other words, allow structures, like strategies, to be learned, beyond being planned. To quote Yokoyama again: "The wiser, though less obvious, approach, is to leave the new design deliberately incomplete. Let life fill in the spaces."[149]

The Design Conundrum

Here is a central conundrum of organization design: when to change a structure that has to be stable? Every structure must eventually settle down—otherwise, how can we call it a structure? But for how long, and how fixed? Organizations are always changing, at least informally, yet they need to fix their structures for a time so that people can get on with their activities—hiring others, buying equipment, programming computers. **People need structure and they need flexibility, but each can obstruct the other.**

The machine organization is inclined to hang on to its structure for as long as possible, until the tension becomes intolerable and it must make the leap to a new structure. The professional organization is even less inclined to restructure, since so much of its structure has been built for the dictates of its professions. The personal and project organizations are the ones inclined to adapt more readily—one at the behest of its chief, the other by the comings and goings of its projects.

Design Doing

Design thinking has become a fashionable phrase of late. On its website, under "What Is Design Thinking?" the renowned design consultancy IDEO has described it as an "iterative process" that proceeds through these phases: empathizing with the users, defining their needs, problems, and own insights, ideating by challenging assumptions and creating ideas for innovative solutions, prototyping to start creating solutions, and testing them.[150]

Why is this called design *thinking* when it reads more like *design doing*, based on *design seeing*—more conversational and evolving than formulaic? As Hannibal said when faced with having to take elephants over the Alps: "I shall either find a way or make one."

The Liberated Unstitution

Finally...I know a seven-year-old who came up with a novel answer to the question posed at the start of this book: "What are these 'organizations' you keep talking about?"[151] When my daughter Susie was seven, she must have been watching me sketching those logos for the original edition of this book, because she suddenly came up with the drawing below. I kept it, no doubt serendipitously for its use right here—a perfect way to end our quest to understand organizations.

Source: Artist Susan Mintzberg, at 7

What do you see? It's a Rorschach, so you can decide for yourself. For me, I see divisions within divisions, each with the head of its leadership lopped off, to release a phoenix-like bird that liberates this "unstitution" from the institution.[152] Is this the organization of the future?

I'm not sure that we shall see such a liberated unstitution any time soon. But I do hope that this book has helped you liberate yourself from the orthodoxies of organizing, so that you can design better organizations in the future. While doing so, please keep in mind these wise words from Alfred North Whitehead: "Seek simplicity and distrust it"...finally!

Notes

Chapter 1

1. Henry Mintzberg, "Time for the Plural Sector," *Stanford Social Innovation Review* 13, no. 3 (2015): 28–33.

2. Frederick Taylor, *Principles of Scientific Management* (Harper & Bro., 1911). "Now, among the various methods and implements used in each element of each trade there is always one method and one implement which is quicker and better than any of the rest. And, this one best method and best implement can only be discovered and developed through a scientific study and analysis of all the methods and implements in use, together with accurate, minute, motion and time study" (p. 25).

3. Published in the mid-1950s in an American professor's bulletin, a Canadian military journal, and *Harper's* magazine, probably based on an anonymous memorandum that circulated in London that was published originally in *Her Majesty's Treasury of the Courts*.

4. Regina E. Herzlingler, "Why Innovation in Health Care Is So Hard," *Harvard Business Review* 84, no. 5 (2006): 58–66.

5. North America, not America, because the sport was invented at my own university, McGill, in Canada. Marc Montgomery, "May 14, 1874. How Canada Created American Football," *Radio Canada International*, May 4, 2015.

6. "Flying Funeral Directors of America," in *The Encyclopaedia of Associations*, Gale Directory Library, 1979.

7. Henry Mintzberg, *Structure in Fives: Designing Effective Organizations* (Prentice-Hall, 1983); Henry Mintzberg, *The Structuring of Organizations: A Synthesis of the Research* (Prentice Hall, 1979).

8. Jean Chevalier and Alain Gheenbrant, *Dictionnaire des Symboles* (Éditions Robert Laffont/JUPITER, 1982).

9. George A. Miller, "The Magic Number Seven, Plus or Minus Two: Some Limits on Our Capacity for Processing Information," *Psychological Review* 63 (1956): 81–97.

10. Mintzberg, *Structuring of Organizations*; Henry Mintzberg, Bruce Ahlstrand, and Joe Lampel, *Strategy Safari: A Guided Tour through the Wilds of Strategic Management* (Free Press and Prentice-Hall, 2009); Henry Mintzberg, *Simply Managing* (Berrett-Koehler, 2013); and Henry Mintzberg, *Rebalancing Society: Radical Renewal beyond Left, Right, and Center* (Berrett-Koehler, 2015).

Chapter 2

11. The company asked not to be named because its promotion had changed. The ad was prepared by Anderson & Lembke, New York.

12. Peter Schein and Edgar H. Schein, *Organizational Culture and Leadership: A Dynamic View* (Wiley & Sons, 1991; first edition by Edgar Schein, 1985).

13. Board directors who seek to exercise direct control over the CEO could be considered *insiders*, while those who act more at arm's length are influencers. If, however, the directors offer advice to the management or raise funds for the organization, they also act like support staff. On stakeholders, see R. Edward Freeman et al., *Stakeholder Theory: The State of the Art* (Cambridge University Press, 2010).

14. Henry Mintzberg, *Power In and Around Organizations* (Prentice Hall, 1983).

15. Michael E. Porter, *Competitive Advantage: Creating and Sustaining Superior Performance* (Free Press, 1985).

16. In correspondence from June 8, 2017, Mark Hammer "distinguish[ed] centripetal and centrifugal organizations." The former, like police forces, tend to gather information but then keep it to themselves, whereas the latter, such as universities, tend to gather information and then distribute it widely.

17. Lise Lamothe, "Le reconfiguration des hôpitaux: Un défi d'ordre professionnel," *Ruptures: Revue transdisciplinaire en santé* 6, no. 2 (1999): 132–148.

18. Various examples can be found in Henry Mintzberg and Ludo Van der Heyden, "Organigraphs: Drawing How Companies Really Work," *Harvard Business Review* (September–October 1999): 87–94; Henry Mintzberg and Ludo Van der Heyden, "Taking a Closer Look. Reviewing the Organization. Is It a Chain, a Hub or a Web?" *Ivey Business Journal* (2000).

19. Sally Helgesen, *The Female Advantage: Women's Ways of Leadership* (Doubleday, 1990), 45–46.

20. Walter Isaacson, *Steve Jobs: The Exclusive Biography* (Little, Brown, 2011).

21. Terry Connolly "On Taking Action Seriously," in G. N. Undon and D. N. Brunstein eds., *Decision-Making: An Interdisciplinary Inquiry* (Kent, 1982): 45

Chapter 3

22. Much of this section is discussed, with extensive examples, in Henry Mintzberg, *Tracking Strategies: Toward a General Theory* (Oxford University Press, 2007).

23. Michael Porter, *Competitive Strategy: Techniques for Analyzing Industries and Competitors* (Free Press, 1980); and Peter F. Drucker, *The Practice of Management* (Harper & Row, 1954).

24. Henri Fayol, *General and Industrial Management* (Paris Institute of Electrical and Electronics Engineering, 1916).

25. What follows is discussed at length, with detailed examples from twenty-nine days in the lives of all kinds of managers, in my books *Managing* (Berrett-Koehler and Pearson, 2009) and, more briefly, *Simply Managing* (Berrett-Koehler, 2013).

26. Michael Porter, "The State of Strategic Thinking," *The Economist,* May 23, 1987, 2.

27. Warren G. Bennis, *On Becoming a Leader* (Basic Books, 2009); and Abraham Zaleznik, "Managers and Leaders: Are They Different?" *Harvard Business Review* (January 2004): 74–81.

28. Herbert Simon, *The Sciences of the Artificial* (MIT Press, 1969).

29. For example, Henry Mintzberg, *The Nature of Managerial Work* (HarperCollins, 1973).

30. See Mintzberg, *Simply Managing*, Chapter 5 for an elaboration of these other conundrums.

31. Ann Langley, "Between 'Paralysis by Analysis' and 'Extention by Instinct'" Sloan Management Review (Spring 1995).

Chapter 4

32. Edward O. Wilson, *Sociobiology: The New Synthesis* (Harvard Belknap Press, 1975), 141.

33. Lars Groth, *Future Organizational Design: The Scope for the IT-based Enterprise* (John Wiley & Sons, 1999), 30.

34. Quoted in Anthony Jay, *Management and Machiavelli* (Bantam Books, 1967), 70.

35. Nizet and Pichault suggested the word "values" "to make it more understandable to ... technically-oriented people" (in personal correspondence). See also Jean Nizet and Francois Pichault, *Introduction à la théorie des configurations : Du « one best way » à la diversité organisationnelle* (De Boeck Supérieur, 2001).

36. This text is adapted from Joseph Lampel and Henry Mintzberg, "Customizing Customization," *Sloan Management Review* (1996): 21–30.

37. Henri Fayol, "Administration industrielle et générale," *Bulletin de la Société de l'Industrie Minérale* 10 (1916); then Luther Gulick and L. Urwick, eds., *Papers on the Science of Administration* (Institute of Public Administration, 1937).

38. Richard Pascale and Anthony Athos, *The Art of Japanese Management* (Viking, 1982).

Chapter 5

39. Adam Smith, *The Wealth of Nations* (1776; J.M. Dent & E.P. Dutton, 1910), 5.

40. Lyndall Urwick, "Public Administration and Scientific Management," *Indian Journal of Public Administration* 2, no. 1 (1956): 41. See also Lyndall Urwick and Luther

Gulick, "Notes on the Theory of Organization," in Gulick and Urwick, *Papers on the Science of Administration*.

41. Alfred Sloan, *My Years with General Motors* (Doubleday & Co., 1963).

42. See Jay Galbraith, *Designing Complex Organizations* (Addison Wesley, 1973), for an excellent discussion of these linkages and an illustration of this continuum.

Chapter 6

43. Mintzberg, *Structuring of Organizations*, 215–297.

44. Harry Braverman, *Labor and Monopoly Capital: The Degradation of Labor* (Monthly Review Press, 1974), 87.

45. In a 1989 article *Fortune* magazine wrote: "What's truly amazing about P&G's historic restructuring is that it is a response to the consumer market, not the stock market." What's truly amazing about this statement is *Fortune*'s use of the phrase "truly amazing."

Chapter 7

46. Isaacson, *Steve Jobs*, 408.

47. Isaacson, *Steve Jobs*, 565. Picture founding CEO Steve Jobs spending his mornings in an Apple laboratory designing product: "He loves coming in here because it's calm and gentle. It's a paradise if you're a visual person. There are no formal design reviews, so there are no huge decision points. Instead, we can make the decisions fluid. Since we iterate every day and never have dumb-ass presentations, we don't run into major disagreements." Isaacson, *Steve Jobs*, 346.

48. Isaacson, *Steve Jobs*, 454.

49. Orvis Collins and David Moore, *The Enterprising Man* (Bureau of Business and Economic Research, Michigan State University, 1964).

Chapter 8

50. The chapter epigraph is from Thomas A. Murphy, interviewed in *Executive* magazine, Cornell Graduate School of Business and Public Administration, Summer 1980.

51. Yuval Noah Hariri, *Sapiens: A Brief History of Humankind* (Random House, 2015), 45.

52. Richard L. A. Sterba, "The Organization and Management of the Temple Corporations in Ancient Mesopotamia," *Academy of Management Review* 1 no. 3 (July 1976): 25.

53. Studs Terkel, *Working: People Talk About What They Do All Day and How They Feel about What They Do* (Pantheon, 1974).

54. Porter, *Competitive Strategy*.

55. "What is the dog there for," *Future Airline Pilot*, January 3, 2013, http://futureair linepilot.blogspot.com/2013/01/what-is-dog-there-for.html.

56. James C. Worthy, *Big Business and Free Men* (Harper & Bros., 1959).

57. Max Weber, *From Max Weber: Essays in Sociology*, edited by Hans Gerth and C. Wright Mills (Oxford University Press, 1958), 214.

58. Pedro Monteiro and Paul S. Adler, "Bureaucracy for the Twenty-First Century:

Clarifying and Expanding Our View of Bureaucratic Organization," *Academy of Management Annals*, 2022, vol. 16, no. 2, 11–12, 16.

59. Michel Crozier, *The Bureaucratic Phenomenon: An Examination of Bureaucracy in Modern Organizations and Its Cultural Setting in France* (University of Chicago Press, 1964).

60. Worthy, *Big Business and Free Men*, 79, 70.

61. Terkel, *Working*, 282.

62. Crozier, *Bureaucratic Phenomenon*, 51.

63. J. C. Spender, *Industry Recipes* (Basil Blackwell, 1989).

64. The box derives from my book *The Rise and Fall of Strategic Planning*.

65. Simon Johnson, "Flat-pack Pioneer Kamprad Built Sweden's IKEA into Global Brand," *Reuters*, January 28, 2018.

Chapter 9

66. F. C. Spencer, "Deductive Reasoning in the Lifelong Continuing Education of a Cardiovascular Surgeon," *Archives of Surgery* 111, no. 11 (November 1976): 1182.

67. Henry Mintzberg, Bruce Ahlstrand, and Joseph Lampel, *Strategy Safari: A Guided Tour through the Wilds of Strategic Management* (Prentice Hall, 1998).

68. Toscanini, quoted in Norman Lebrecht, *The Maestro Myth: Great Conductors in Pursuit of Power* (Simon & Schuster, 1991), chapter 4. The Orpheus Chamber Orchestra "is known for its collaborative musical style in which the musicians, not a conductor, interpret the score." Orpheus Chamber Orchestra, https://orpheusnyc.org.

69. Henry Mintzberg, *Managing the Myths of Health Care: The Separations between Care, Cure, Control, and Community* (Berrett-Kohler, 2017), 52–60 and 157–162.

70. For a brilliant illustration of this third problem, see Atul Gawande, "The Health Care Bell Curve," *The New Yorker*, December 6, 2004.

71. Henry Mintzberg and Susan Mintzberg, "Looking Down versus Reaching Out: The University in the 21st Century," in progress, 2022.

72. Sholom Glouberman and Henry Mintzberg, "Managing the Care of Health and the Cure of Disease—Part I: Differentiation," *Health Care Management Review* 26, no. 1 (Winter 2001): 56–69.

73. Mintzberg, *Managing the Myths of Health Care*, Part I.

74. For further detail, see "A Note on the Unionization of Professionals from the Perspective of Organization Theory," *Industrial Relations Law Journal* (now known as *Berkeley Journal of Employment and Labor Law*) (1983).

Chapter 10

75. A. A. Milne, *Winnie-the-Pooh* (Methuen, 1926). By the way, have another look at the Milne quote. He wrote a clever little trick in there that nobody I know has ever noticed. (I discovered it by mistake, trying to recall the quote from memory.) Stuck? Look at the word *one*.

76. I struggled with the second label for this form, going through *pioneer* and *prospector* (Raymond E. Miles and Charles C. Snow, *Organizational Strategy, Structure, and*

Process [McGraw-Hill, 1978]) *customizer* and *innovator* (Clay Christensen, *The Innovator's Dilemma: When New Technologies Cause Great Firms to Fail* [Harvard Business Review Press, 1997]) before finally settling back on *pioneer*. But any one would have done.

77. Keidel has written extensively about sports as models of different organizations, with conclusions similar to that in this book about baseball, football, and basketball. See his *Game Plans: Sports Strategies for Business* (Beard Books, 1985); also see his "Teamwork, PC Style," *PC/Computing* 2, no. 7 (July 1989): 126–131, and "Team Sports Models As a Generic Organizational Framework," *Human Relations* 40, no. 9 (1987): 591–612.

78. In a seminar I gave to government administrators in Australia, one frustrated head of a public park, who had had enough of the pressures of the government technocrats, suggested I add a label to go along with the bureaucracies and the adhocracies. He called it *hypocracy*—namely, to say one thing while doing another, such as centralizing in the name of decentralization.

79. Henry Mintzberg, "Organization Design: Fashion or Fit," *Harvard Business Review* (January–February 1981): 103–116.

80. Frank Martela, "What Makes Self-Managing Organizations Novel? Comparing How Weberian Bureaucracy, Mintzberg's Adhocracy, and Self-Organizing Solve Six Fundamental Problems of Organizing," *Journal of Organizational Design* 8, no. 1 (December 2019): 1–23.

81. Mintzberg, *Tracking Strategies*, 82–83.

82. George Huber, "Organizational Information Systems: Determinants of Their Performance and Behavior," *Management Science* 28, no. 2 (February 1982) 138–155; Rolf A. Lundin and Anders Söderholm, "A Theory of the Temporary Organization," *Scandinavian Journal of Management* 11, no. 4 (1995): 437–455; Charles A. O'Reilly III and Michael L. Tushman, "The Ambidextrous Organization," *Harvard Business Review* (April 2004): 74–81; Terje Grønning, *Working without a Boss: Lattice Organization with Direct Person-to-Person Communication at WL Gore & Associates, Inc.* (SAGE Publications: SAGE Business Cases Originals, 2016); Raymond E. Miles and Charles C. Snow, "The New Network Firm: A Spherical Structure Built on a Human Investment Philosophy," *Organizational Dynamics* 23, no. 4 (1995): 5–20; and James B. Quinn and Penny C. Paquette, "Technology in Services: Creating Organizational Revolutions," *MIT Sloan Management Review* (Winter 1990): 67–77.

Chapter 11

83. Sterba, "Organization and Management of the Temple Corporation in Ancient Mesopotamia," 18.

84. Monteiro and Adler recently published a major review of the bureaucratic organization, referring to its "continuing presence as the predominant organizational form." "Bureaucracy for the 21st Century: Clarifying and Expanding Our View of Bureaucratic Organization," *Academy of Management Annals*, 2022, vol. 16, no. 2, p. 427.

85. Henry Mintzberg, *The Rise and Fall of Strategic Planning* (Free Press, 2003).

86. Henry Mintzberg and Janet Rose, "Strategic Management Upside Down: A

Study of McGill University from 1829 to 1980," *Canadian Journal of Administrative Sciences* (December 2003): 270–290.

87. Mintzberg and Rose, "Strategic Management Upside Down."

88. Henry Mintzberg and Alexandra McHugh, "Strategy Formation in an Adhocracy," *Administrative Science Quarterly* (1985); also Mintzberg, *Tracking Strategies*, chapter 4.

89. Mintzberg, "Managing Exceptionally," *Organization Science* 12, no. 6 (December 2001): 759–771. Also discussed in Mintzberg, *Managing* and *Simply Managing*.

90. Mintzberg, *Managing the Myths of Health Care*, 196–197.

91. Andy Grove, *High Output Management* (Pan, 1985).

Chapter 13

92. I first used the term *communityship* in an article in the *Financial Times*: "Community-ship Is the Answer," *Financial Times*, October 23, 2006, 8. On "collective spirit," see Henry Mintzberg, "Rebuilding Companies as Communities," *Harvard Business Review* (July–August 2009).

93. Robert R. Locke, *The Collapse of the American Management Mystique* (Oxford University Press, 1987), 179.

94. Philip Selznick, *Leadership in Administration: A Sociological Interpretation* (Harper & Row, 1957).

95. Colin Hales, "'Bureaucracy-lite' and Continuities in Managerial Work," *British Journal of Management* 13, no. 1 (March 2002): 51.

96. Francis Macdonald Cornford, *Microcosmographia Academica: Being a Guide for the Young Academic Politician* (Bowes and Bowes, 1908), available online. https://www.cs.kent.ac.uk/people/staff/iau/cornford/cornford.html.

97. Martin Lindauer, *Communication among Social Bees* (Harvard University Press, 1961), 43.

98. Adapted from Mintzberg, *Power In and Around Organizations*, 187–217.

Chapter 14

99. James O'Toole and Warren Bennis, "Our Federalist Future: The Leadership Imperative," *Center for Effective Organizations Publications* 92, no. 9 (1992). Available online.

100. R. P. Rumelt, *Strategy, Structure, and Economic Performance* (Harvard University Press, 1974), 21.

101. O'Toole and Bennis, "Our Federalist Future," 79.

102. Tarun Khanna and Krishna Palepu ("Why Focused Strategies May Be Wrong for Emerging Markets," *Harvard Business Review* [July–August 1997]) attribute the success of conglomerates in emerging markets to the provision by the holding company of institutional supports that are otherwise lacking in those countries. Ramachandran, Manikandan, and Pant, in contrast, attribute the success of conglomerates outside the US to the legally independent status of the business, each with its own board of directors, yet a "a high level of involvement between ownership and management," sometimes with substantial ownership in the central company, whose executives may sit on those boards

(J. Ramachandran, K. S. Manikandan, and Anirvan Pant, "Why Conglomerates Thrive [Outside the U.S.]," *Harvard Business Review* [December 2013]).

103. Alfred D. Chandler, *The Visible Hand: The Managerial Revolution in American Business* (Harvard University Press, 1977), 82.

104. Joseph L. Bower, "Planning within the Firm," *The American Economic Review, Papers and Proceedings of the 82nd Annual Conference* (May 1970): 186–194.

105. Sumantra Ghoshal and I published an article titled "'Diversifiction and Diversifact': What a Difference an 'a' Can Make," *California Management Review* 3 (Fall 1994).

106. If you climb a mountain road on a bicycle and come straight back down, you have done exactly as much uphill as downhill, right? Not quite. You have done as much *distance*, but you have spent far more *time*. What matters to you more while climbing on a bicycle—the distance or the time?

107. Ely Devons's account of statistics and planning in the Air Ministry of the British Government during World War II is a brilliant description of the litany of horrors that can result from mindless counting. See Devons, *Planning in Practice: Essays in Aircraft Planning in War-Time* (Cambridge University Press, 1950), chapter 7.

108. Henry Mintzberg, "A Note on That Dirty Word Efficiency," *Interfaces* 12, no. 5 (October 1982): 101–105, https://www.jstor.org/stable/25060327.

109. Robert S. Kaplan and David P. Norton, "The Balanced Scorecard—Measures That Drive Performance," *Harvard Business Review* (January–February 1992): 71–79.

Chapter 15

110. D. L. Sills, *The Volunteers* (The Free Press, 1957).

111. Maurice Maeterlinck, *The Life of the Bee* (Cornell University Press, 1901), 32.

112. Myrada, https://myrada.org, accessed May 16, 2022.

113. Mitz Noda, "The Japanese Way," *Executive* (Summer 1980).

114. James Surowiecki, *The Wisdom of Crowds* (Anchor, 2005), xii.

115. Irving L. Janis, *Groupthink: Psychological Studies of Policy Decisions and Fiascoes* (Houghton Mifflin, 1982).

116. Weick quoted in Robert M. Randall, "Sniping at Strategic Planning," *Planning Review* 12, no. 3 (May 1984): 11.

Part VI

117. Charles Darwin to J. D. Hooker, August 1, 1857.

118. This term was coined by Lex Donaldson, who wrote his criticism of configuration theory (lumping) at length, in "For Cartesianism: Against Organizational Types and Quantum Jumps," in *For Positivist Organisation Theory: Proving the Hard Core* (Sage, 1996). See also Harold D. Doty, William H. Glick, and George P. Huber, "Fit, Equifinality, and Organizational Effectiveness: A Test of Two Configurational Theories," in the *Academy of Management Journal* 36, no. 6 (1993); as well as that of Krabberød, who analyzed the pros and cons of Doty, Glick, and Huber's study: Tommy Krabberød, "Standing on the Shoulders of Giants? Exploring Consensus on the Validity Status of Mintzberg's Configuration Theory after a Negative Test," *SAGE Open* 5, no. 4 (October 2015).

Chapter 17

119. Danny Miller, *The Icarus Paradox: How Exceptional Companies Bring about Their Own Downfall* (HarperCollins, 1992).

120. Miller, *Icarus Paradox*, 4.

121. Danny Miller and Manfred F. R. Kets de Vries, *The Neurotic Organization: Diagnosis and Revitalizing Unhealthy Companies* (HarperCollins, 1991).

Chapter 18

122. Ray Raphael, *Edges: Human Ecology of the Backcountry* (Alfred A. Knopf, 1976), 5–6.

123. See the description of a bureau-adhocracy in Arlyne Bailey and Eric H. Nielsen, "Creating a Bureau-Adhocracy: Integrating Standardized and Innovative Services in a Professional Work Group," *Human Relations* 45, no. 7 (1992): 687–710.

Chapter 19

124. Thomas Peters and Robert H. Waterman, *In Search of Excellence: Lessons from America's Best-Run Companies* (HarperCollins, 1982).

125. Peters and Waterman's hugely successful book, *In Search of Excellence*, described some exceptional corporations that managed to endure with excellence, perhaps because they maintained compelling cultures. But this book might have been their undoing: with all that attention, not long after the book appeared, the fortunes of some of them were reversed (as discussed in a famous *Business Week* article titled "OOPS!" November 5, 1984). For how remarkably stable the structure of a university can be, see our study of McGill University across 150 years: "Strategic Management Upside Down."

126. Transition to the Divisional Form does not change the machine structure so much as extrapolate it, while culture and conflict can be considered forces that facilitate or provoke these three changes in structure.

127. On internal corporate venturing, see Robert Burgelman, "A Process Model of Internal Corporate Venturing in the Diversified Major Firm," *Administrative Science Quarterly* 28, no. 2 (June 1983): 223–244; and Edward Zajac, Brian R. Golden, and Stephen M. Shortell, "New Organizational Forms for Enhancing Innovation: The Case of Internal Corporate Joint Ventures," *Management Science* 37, no. 2 (February 1991): 170–184.

128. For a discussion of these last two, see Charles O'Reilly III and Michael Tushman, "The Ambidextrous Organization," *Harvard Business Review* 82, no. 4 (April 2004): 74–81.

129. Emi Osono, Norihiko Shimizu, and Hirotaka Takeuchi, *Extreme Toyota: Radical Contradictions That Drive Success at the World's Best Manufacturer* (John Wiley & Sons, Inc., 2008), 98.

130. For a further discussion of the separations in hospitals between care, cure, control, and community, see Glouberman and Mintzberg, "Managing the Care of Health and the Cure of Disease," especially parts I and II; see also Mintzberg, *Managing the Myths of Health Care*.

131. This has been described in our research on the history of the Volkswagenwerk: Henry Mintzberg, "Patterns in Strategy Formation," *Management Science* 24, no. 9 (May 1978): 934–948. See also Mintzberg, *Tracking Strategies*, especially chapter 2.

132. Joseph Schumpeter, *Capitalism, Socialism and Democracy* (Harper & Brothers, 1942).

Chapter 20

133. Some of the sources consulted here include Groth, *Future Organizational Design*; Filipe M. Santos and Kathleen M. Eisenhardt, "Organizational Boundaries and Theories of Organization," *Organization Science* 16, no. 5 (September–October 2005): 491–508; Henry Chesbrough, "Business Model Innovation: It's Not Just About Technology Anymore," *Strategy & Leadership* 35, no. 6 (November 2007): 12–17; M.D.L. Seidel and K. J. Stewart, "An Initial Description of the C-form," *Research in the Sociology of Organizations* 33 (November 2011): 37–72; Phanish Puranam, Oliver Alexy, and Markus Reitzig, "What's 'New' about New Forms of Organizing?" *Academy of Management Review* 39, no. 2 (2014): 162–180; Annabelle Gawer and Michael Cusumano, "Business Platforms," in *International Encyclopedia of the Social & Behavioral Sciences,* 2nd ed. (Elsevier, 2015); Michael G. Jacobides, Carmelo Cennamo, and Annabelle Gawer, "Towards a Theory of Ecosystems," *Strategic Management Journal* 39, no. 8 (May 2018): 2255–2276; and Andrew Shipilov and Annabelle Gawer, "Integrating Research on Interorganizational Networks and Ecosystems," *Academy of Management Annals* 14 no. 1 (January 2020): 92–121. They are listed together here because many do not fit neatly into one or other of the categories used in this chapter.

134. Carol W. Gelderman et al., "Henry Ford," in *Encyclopaedia Britannica*, www .britannica.com/biography/Henry-Ford, 2022.

135. Groth, *Future Organizational Design*, 166.

136. Victor-Adrian Troacă and Dumitru-Alexandru Bodislav, "Outsourcing. The Concept," *Theoretical and Applied Economics* 19, no. 6 (2012): 51–58.

137. C. K. Prahalad and Gary Hamel, "The Core Competence of the Corporation," *Harvard Business Review* (May–June 1990): 79–91; also C. K. Prahalad and Gary Hamel, *Competing for the Future* (Harvard Business Review Press, 1996).

138. Henry W. Chesbrough and Melissa M. Appleyard, "Open Innovation and Strategy," *California Management Review* 50, no. 1 (Fall 2007): 22.

139. BioNTech chief executive Ugur Sahin and his wife, Oezlem Tuereci. Ludwig Burger and Patricia Weiss, "Behind Pfizer's Vaccine, an Understated Husband-and-Wife: 'Dream Team,'" *Reuters*, November 9, 2020.

140. Seidel and Stewart, "Initial Description of the C-form."

141. It has been suggested that such users be called "complementors" rather than suppliers. See Shipilov and Gawer, "Integrating Research on Interorganizational Networks and Ecosystems."

142. Hence Benoît Demil and Xavier Lecocq refer to "bazaar governance—based on a specific legal contract: the open licence" in "Neither Market nor Hierarchy nor Network:

The Emergence of Bazaar Governance," *Organization Studies* 27, no. 10 (October 2006): 1447.

143. Göran Ahrne and Nils Brunsson, "Organizations and Meta-organizations," *Scandinavian Journal of Management* 21, no. 4 (2005): 429–449.

144. Among the topics of CoachingOurselves.com related to this book are "Developing Our Organization as a Community," "Silos and Slabs in Organizations," "Virtual Teams," "Political Games in Organizations," and "Management Styles: Art, Craft, Science."

Chapter 21

145. Simon, *Sciences of the Artificial*, 55.

146. Jeanne Liedtka and Henry Mintzberg, "Time for Design," *Design Management Review* (Spring 2006).

147. Peters and Waterman, *In Search of Excellence, 108*, from Gordon Siu https:// ejstrategy.wordpress.com/2011/04/19/sbb-bees-and-flies-making-strategy/.

148. Yoshinori Yokoyama, "An Architect Looks at Organization Design," *McKinsey Quarterly* no. 4 (Autumn 1992): 126.

149. Yokoyama, "Architect Looks at Organization Design," 122.

150. "How Do People Define Design Thinking," IDEO, https://designthinking.ideo .com/faq/how-do-people-define-design-thinking (accessed August 30, 2021).

151. So did Yuval Harari: "Microsoft isn't the buildings it owns, the people it employs, the shareholders it serves—rather, it is an intricate legal fiction woven by lawmakers and lawyers." From his book *21 Lessons for the 21st Century* (Spiegel & Grau, 2018), 248.

152. See Unstitution's LinkedIn page at www.linkedin.com/company/unstitution.

Index

Illustrations and tables are denoted by page numbers in *italics*. Page numbers followed by n indicate note number.

About the Author

Henry Mintzberg is a writer, researcher, and educator, most of whose work focuses on managing organizations, developing managers, and (most recently) rebalancing societies. This is his twenty-first book; the others have earned him twenty-one honorary degrees. Henry sits (a) in the Cleghorn Chair of Management Studies (b) in the Desautels Faculty of Management (c) at McGill University (d) in Montreal, Canada. While devoting his professional life to studying, experiencing, and coping with organizations, he has been spending his private life escaping from them—in a canoe (where he collects beaver sculptures), up mountains, and on skates, snowshoes, and a bicycle. Henry cherishes one partner, two daughters, and three grandchildren. (For more, see mintzberg.org, also RebalancingSociety.org.)

❋ Berrett–Koehler
BK̄ Publishers

Berrett-Koehler is an independent publisher dedicated to an ambitious mission: *Connecting people and ideas to create a world that works for all.*

Our publications span many formats, including print, digital, audio, and video. We also offer online resources, training, and gatherings. And we will continue expanding our products and services to advance our mission.

We believe that the solutions to the world's problems will come from all of us, working at all levels: in our society, in our organizations, and in our own lives. Our publications and resources offer pathways to creating a more just, equitable, and sustainable society. They help people make their organizations more humane, democratic, diverse, and effective (and we don't think there's any contradiction there). And they guide people in creating positive change in their own lives and aligning their personal practices with their aspirations for a better world.

And we strive to practice what we preach through what we call "The BK Way." At the core of this approach is *stewardship,* a deep sense of responsibility to administer the company for the benefit of all of our stakeholder groups, including authors, customers, employees, investors, service providers, sales partners, and the communities and environment around us. Everything we do is built around stewardship and our other core values of *quality, partnership, inclusion,* and *sustainability.*

This is why Berrett-Koehler is the first book publishing company to be both a B Corporation (a rigorous certification) and a benefit corporation (a for-profit legal status), which together require us to adhere to the highest standards for corporate, social, and environmental performance. And it is why we have instituted many pioneering practices (which you can learn about at www.bkconnection.com), including the Berrett-Koehler Constitution, the Bill of Rights and Responsibilities for BK Authors, and our unique Author Days.

We are grateful to our readers, authors, and other friends who are supporting our mission. We ask you to share with us examples of how BK publications and resources are making a difference in your lives, organizations, and communities at www.bkconnection.com/impact.

Dear reader,

Thank you for picking up this book and welcome to the worldwide BK community! You're joining a special group of people who have come together to create positive change in their lives, organizations, and communities.

What's BK all about?

Our mission is to connect people and ideas to create a world that works for all.

Why? Our communities, organizations, and lives get bogged down by old paradigms of self-interest, exclusion, hierarchy, and privilege. But we believe that can change. That's why we seek the leading experts on these challenges—and share their actionable ideas with you.

A welcome gift

To help you get started, we'd like to offer you a **free copy** of one of our bestselling ebooks:

www.bkconnection.com/welcome

When you claim your **free ebook**, you'll also be subscribed to our blog.

Our freshest insights

Access the best new tools and ideas for leaders at all levels on our blog at ideas.bkconnection.com.

Sincerely,

Your friends at Berrett-Koehler

Certified

Corporation